CRUISING THE WESTERN MEDITERRANEAN

CONTENTS

INTRODUCTION	3
PREPARING TO CRUISE	4
THE BIG PICTURE	8
THE LAY OF THE LAND	12
MAJOR PORTS OF CALL IN FRANCE	18
* Marseille	18
* Nice (Côte d'Azur)	21
* Saint Tropez	24
MAJOR PORT OF CALL IN GIBRALTAR	37
* Gibraltar	37
MAJOR PORTS OF CALL IN MOROCCO	46
* Casablanca	50
* Marrakesh	54
* Tangier	55
MAJOR PORT OF CALL IN PORTUGAL	71
* Lisbon	73
* Portimão (Algarve)	78
MAJOR PORTS OF CALL IN SPAIN	95

* **Barcelona**	**101**
* **València**	**116**
* **Cartagena**	**122**
* **Málaga**	**137**
* **Granada**	**141**
* **Palma de Majorca**	**155**
* **Ibiza**	**159**
* **Cadiz**	**166**
* **Seville**	**169**
FINAL WRAP UP	**182**
ABOUT THE AUTHOR	**183**

All Wikimedia.com photographs used in this book where I do not have my own contain the name of the author or copyright holder and are herein used in accordance with Creative Commons Attribution Share Alike license 2.0, 3.0 or 4.0.

The majority of maps used in this book is from Open Street Map contributors and are so noted for each map. For further information contact: www.OpenStreetMap.org/copyright

INTRODUCTION

The Mediterranean Sea is one of the most visited parts of the world. Tourists from all continents come to enjoy its beautiful shores, sandy beaches combined with the antiquities that represent the first great civilizations on earth. Essentially the Mediterranean can be called the Cradle of Western Civilization, having been home to the ancient Egyptians, Phoenicians, Israelites, Hittites, Greeks and Romans to name the most obvious. Today it is home to a diversity of nations representing southern Europe, Asia Minor and the shores of North Africa.

This great body of water, which covers 970,000 square miles or 2,500,000 square kilometers is technically an extension of the Atlantic Ocean. But people who both live around its shores and visitors alike consider it to be akin to an inland ocean in its own right.

To create a book for those who wish to have a better understanding of the lands and peoples of the Mediterranean involves so many diverse landscapes and cultures, that it became necessary to divide the text into three separate books. This first volume covers the countries that border the northern and southern shores of the western part of the Mediterranean Basin. The book is not meant to serve as a pocket guide that you would carry with you while on shore. Its purpose is to provide you with geographic, historic and cultural detail regarding the major ports of southern France, Malta, northern Morocco, Portugal and Spain visited by cruise ships on a variety of itineraries. Each chapter will be devoted to a particular port, grouped alphabetically by both country and port of call. There will be information as to local customs, notations on how to interact with locals, where to go and what to see. Unlike the popular "guidebooks" on the market, these books are not filled with shopping locations, restaurant information, opening hours of major venues and other tidbits that you would expect in a guidebook. Rather you will learn about each country and the ports of call with reference to their overall geographic setting, physical layout, ease or difficulty of getting around, public safety and the worthiness of major historic and cultural sites. The information provided will make you a better traveler and give you the confidence to know you are getting the most value out of your experience.

Dr. Lew Deitch,
March 2017

PREPARING TO CRUISE

For residents of North America in particular, the Mediterranean is thought of as the most exotic and exciting part of Europe, also affording an opportunity on some cruise itineraries to touch on either Asia Minor or North Africa. People visualize the bright blue waters, rugged landscapes, whitewashed villages and plenty of sunshine as providing for the perfect vacation. Although some expectations may be too high, most find that when the visit they are not disappointed. And many tens of thousands of people return for further travels in this part of the world.

This volume has been prepared for those who are planning a cruise where the major portion of the itinerary will be centered upon the ports of the western part of the Mediterranean Sea. As previously noted, it is designed to provide you with geographic and historic information so that you become better informed about the major places you will be visiting. But unlike a traditional guidebook, it is not designed to provide restaurant or hotel listings or advice on specific places to shop.

What do you need to do to prepare for your cruise? This question involves numerous sub topics that will be explained. There are many questions people have regarding visas, the flights, what to pack with regard to weather conditions, currency issues and health concerns. I will address many of those issues here. If you have specific and personalized questions, please contact me at my web page through the "Ask Doctor Lew" page. I will respond with answers to your personal questions. The web site is http://www.doctorlew.com.

VISAS: For citizens holding United States, Canadian or European Union passports, you will not require a visa to visit any of the countries in the western portion of the Mediterranean Sea. But you will need to have a valid passport that still has at least six months left before its expiration date.

FLIGHTS TO AND FROM THE SHIP: Most of the cruises in the western portion of the Mediterranean Sea will either begin or terminate in the ports of Civitavecchia (Rome), Barcelona, Málaga or Lisbon. For those who live within the European Union, these cities are accessible by either air or rail with minimal difficulty. And most can be accessed from the majority of hub cities within a matter of a few hours. For those coming from North America, the major hub airports in the region include Rome, Barcelona or Lisbon where several airlines offer direct flights from North America and returning. The larger airports of London Heathrow, Frankfurt and Paris will each offer easy connecting flights to or from the ship.

WEATHER: As previously noted the Mediterranean climate is one in which the winter weather is cool and often rainy, but with variations from one year to the next. Daytime high temperatures will be in the 70's Fahrenheit (between 20 and 25 Celsius) with occasional periods of warmer daytime highs. Rain comes in blustery cold front storms that sweep in from the Atlantic Ocean and will generally last for less than a full day. On rare occasions, cold winds and rain or snow can sweep down from northern Europe, but these conditions are generally most unlikely. If you do go on a tour into the interior of Spain, especially to Granada, it can often be quite chilly even during the day.

Summer in the Mediterranean can be very hot and is most often quite dry. Daytime highs will be in the 80's Fahrenheit (30's Celsius) and there are heat waves where temperatures can reach over 100 Fahrenheit (low 40's Celsius). Hot winds can sometimes blow in from across the sea, bringing desiccating Sahara like conditions. There are occasional thunderstorms during summer, especially in the mountainous regions.

The ideal times to cruise the Mediterranean are during late spring into early summer and then again late summer into the autumn months. During these times, the weather is balmy with temperatures in the low 70's Fahrenheit (low 20's Celsius), light breezes and plenty of sunshine. It is one of the most beautiful times of the year. And the nights can be just slightly nippy.

WHAT TO PACK: You will be well advised to pack light clothes for the spring and summer months, preferably cotton in pastel colors, as they breathe easier and help keep you cool. If you are prone to any adverse reaction to heat or sunlight, a comfortable hat is recommended. And it is also wise to have a good sunscreen. And during the evenings it does get surprisingly cool at night and a light sweater or long sleeve shirt is recommended. At times springtime days can still be quite cool up until around noon.

During fall and winter, long sleeves and long pants are preferable along with a medium weight jacket and a sweater than can be worn underneath if it should get moderately cold. Layers help best during winter and if you have at least two sweaters and a warm scarf, you will be prepared for the coldest conditions.

Depending upon your cruise line, you may need formal or smart casual dress for evening events on board. This of course varies with each cruise operator. And attending such evening events is always optional.

On deck, a light sweater or windbreaker is advisable even during summer. During winter it can sometimes be quite chilly on deck, so your warmer sweaters or jackets will come in quite handy. Remember that when the ship is in motion, there is always going to be a relatively stiff breeze coming across the bow and forward decks.

FOOD AND WATER: In the western portion of the Mediterranean you will have few concerns about food and water while in France, Spain, Malta or Portugal. Both countries maintain high sanitation standards. But just to play safe, it is always best to drink bottled water. As for eating raw vegetables, salads and fruits, you should be fine so long as you are eating in reputable restaurants where high standards are maintained. However, if your ship is calling into ports such as Tangiers or Casablanca, you should absolutely be careful about making certain you only drink bottled water. As for eating raw vegetables, salads and fruits, you will be relatively safe in major hotels and five-star restaurants. Otherwise I recommend that you refrain from eating anything that has not been cooked and served hot.

HEALTH CONCERNS: There are no major health concerns that should impact you as a visitor. But as a precaution, I always carry two prescription items that I consider the traveler's best friends. Have your doctor prescribe Lomotil, which is used in cases where you have lower intestinal upsets that can happen to anyone from simply eating unfamiliar foods. But if your lower bowel upset comes with fever, chills or a generally sick feeling, it is more likely the result of some type of bacterial inflammation. Then you should take Cipro, an antibiotic especially for lower digestive bacterial conditions. Your doctor will explain the use of Cipro, or if in doubt, ask the ship's doctor.

Always take out a traveler's health insurance policy before departure from home. And make certain that you have a sizable allowance for medical evacuation. This is just a normal precaution when traveling far from home. Hospitals in all of the European countries you will be visiting meet exceptionally high standards with regard to their services and the levels of sanitation. Hospitals in Morocco may not meet our western expectations.

CURRENCY: The official currency of France, Spain, Malta and Portugal is the Euro. The currency of Gibraltar is the Gibraltar Pound. If you visit Morocco, the official currency is the Dirham, however, if Tangiers is your sole port of call, most local merchants will accept the Euro. My recommendation is to order small amounts of local currency from your bank at home prior to departure.

POSTAGE: If you wish to send post cards or letters you are best doing it on board the ship. It is easier than attempting to find local post offices, navigate the language barriers and waste valuable time otherwise better spent sightseeing.

CRIME: In the western part of the Mediterranean you will find that street crime other than pickpocketing is relatively rare. As for your money, passport or other valuables, you should guard them at all times anywhere in the world that you travel. I do not advise taking a passport with when you go ashore unless it is absolutely necessary, which is the case in some countries where you need to clear local immigration after leaving the ship. Within the European Union, that is generally not necessary. And in Morocco, any clearance needed is done on board ship. When it comes to pickpockets, the only city in this part of the Mediterranean in which it is quite rampant is Barcelona. So keep your money and credit cards either in a front pocket or inside money pouch. The Metro and Las Ramblas in Barcelona do have the reputation for pickpockets roaming quite freely.

Here are some rules that I recommend to be observed in any region that will make your journey safe and successful:

* When out in public, do not wear expensive jewelry or watches.

* Do not flash large amounts of money when making a purchase.

* Keep money, passport or other valuable documents well hidden, using an inside pouch or money belt.

* Do not carry large handbags.

* Keep cameras close, preferably worn around your neck.

* If using public trains, pay the extra fee to ride in first class carriages.

These recommendations may sound a bit intimidating, but they are good precautions to follow. People throughout the western Mediterranean are friendly and helpful to visitors. Likewise in Morocco, you will find that locals are very receptive and friendly to tourists. But remember that you are in an Islamic country, so proper moderate dress is advised. And when in public, keep a low profile and do not call attention to yourselves.

THE BIG PICTURE

The vast Mediterranean Sea

From the Straits of Gibraltar to the Black Sea, the Mediterranean Sea stretches over three time zones, a distance of over 2,300 miles or 3,700 kilometers. It reaches a maximum depth of over 16,890 feet or 5,148 meters. At its widest point the Mediterranean is just over 990 miles or 1,600 kilometers, stretching north from Libya to the upper part of Italy.

When you look at a map of any large body of water such as the ocean or a major sea like the Mediterranean, you will notice that we humans are not content unless even smaller portions are given individual names. A sea as large as the Mediterranean can be subdivided into smaller seas, bays, gulfs, sounds, straits and any number of geographic names to enable each local feature to be given its own reference. The major sub names used in the Mediterranean include:

* Straits of Gibraltar - The narrow opening into the Mediterranean from the Atlantic Ocean, separating southern Spain and Gibraltar from Morocco in North Africa.

* Alboran Sea - The narrow portion of the Mediterranean inside from the Straits of Gibraltar separating Spain from North Africa.

* Balearic Sea - That part of the Mediterranean between the east coast of Spain and the offshore Balearic Islands.

* Tyrrhenian Sea - That portion of the Mediterranean between the west coast of Italy and the two large offshore islands of Corsica and Sardinia
* Ligurian Sea - That small portion of the Mediterranean between the coast of France and the island of Corsica
* Adriatic Sea - That portion of the Mediterranean between the east coast of Italy and the Balkan States of what was formerly Yugoslavia.
* Ionian Sea - That wider portion of the Mediterranean south of the Adriatic that separates the southern boot of Italy from the mainland of Greece.
* Gulf of Sidra - That part of the Mediterranean that appears to take a bite out of Libya's coastline.
* Aegean Sea - That portion of the Mediterranean between the eastern coast of Greece and the west coast of Turkey, containing the hundreds of islands that are primarily part of Greece.
* Sea of Crete - The portion of the Mediterranean south of the cluster of small Greek islands in the Aegean Sea and the island of Crete.
*Dardanelle Straits - The narrow body of water leading from the eastern Mediterranean toward the Black Sea.
* Sea of Marmara - The small almost landlocked sea that is east of the Dardanelle Straits leading into the Bosporus Straits.
* Bosporus Straits - The narrow channel leading from the Sea of Marmara into the Black Sea.

There are many countries that surround the Mediterranean Sea, lying on what are recognized as three separate continents. However, in geographic reality Europe and Asia are in actuality one continent better referred to as Eurasia. And there is a narrow neck of land called the Sinai Peninsula that connects Africa to Eurasia. Portugal is often considered to be a Mediterranean country, yet it lies outside of the Straits of Gibraltar. Its culture and landscape are part of the Iberian Peninsula that also includes Spain. And so many Mediterranean features such as climate and vegetation exist in Portugal thus essentially making it a Mediterranean country. Morocco is part Mediterranean, yet most of its coastline is along the Atlantic Ocean. Egypt fronts on the Mediterranean, but it also has an equally long coastline along the Red Sea while its interior is a part of the Sahara Desert.

The climate of the entire landmass surrounding the sea is essentially arid to semi-arid with summer being the dry season. This particular type of climate with cool, wet winters and hot, dry summers bordering the sea in the latitude range of 30 to 40 degrees north or south on the west sides of continents has become recognized as a Mediterranean Climate (Cfa under the Köppen Climatic Classification). The landscape is generally one of short grasses and scrub woodlands with trees that are often gnarled and have leathery leaves that exude sticky oils to protect them from summer desiccation. Brush fires are often a major problem for people living in foothill regions.

From a cultural perspective, there are few major world-class cities that border the Mediterranean Sea, and only eight national capitals are located along the sea, with the majority being inland cities. Here is a list of the Mediterranean countries starting in the west and going clockwise around the northern shore to Turkey and then returning to the west along the Asia Minor and North African shores. You can use the map at the start of this chapter for reference:
* Portugal (actually an Atlantic nation) with its capital Lisbon on the Atlantic Ocean.
* Spain with its capital Madrid located in the interior.
* France with its capital Paris well to the north.
* Principality of Monaco with its capital Monte Carlo on the sea.
* Italy with its capital Rome just inland a short distance from the sea.
* Slovakia with its capital Ljubljana in the interior mountains.
* Croatia with its capital of Zagreb well to the interior.
* Montenegro with its capital of Podgorica in the interior.
* Albania with its capital Tirana in the interior.
* Greece with its capital Athens on the sea
* Turkey with its capital Ankara in the interior high plateau.
* Cyprus with its capital Nicosia in the middle of the island.
* Turkish Republic of North Cyprus with its capital Lefkosia in the middle of the island, actually the northern half of the city of Nicosia.
* Syria with its capital of Damascus well to the interior.
* Lebanon with its capital Beirut on the sea
* Israel with its capital Jerusalem a short distance inland
* Egypt with its capital Cairo located over 100 miles south along the Nile River.
* Libya with its capital Tripoli on the sea.
* Malta with its capital Valletta on the sea.
* Tunisia with its capital Tunis on the sea.
* Algeria with its capital Algiers on the sea
* Morocco with its capital Rabat on the Atlantic Ocean.

The Mediterranean Sea region has contributed so much to the world with regard to being the incubator of Western Civilization. What began in Mesopotamia spread to Egypt and the Anatolian Plateau of modern day Turkey. In these areas the rudiments of agriculture, animal husbandry, the development of cities, government, writing and mathematics ultimately spread to Greece where a golden age of architecture, science, literature and philosophy formed the foundations of our contemporary Western world. Rome took from Greece and built upon it, giving us a further foundation upon which to build or present day lives, though with the interruption of what became the Dark Ages. But then the Renaissance and Baroque Eras developed around the shores of the Mediterranean.

Today the Western world values the Mediterranean for its beauty, its diverse cultures, its good (and essentially healthy) cuisine and its overall lifestyle. Many millions as the garden spot of the world often think this of.

THE LAY OF THE LAND

The landscape is essentially the stage upon which the human drama of settlement takes place. To fully appreciate any region you visit, you must first have a good understanding of the natural geography, the plains, mountains, rivers, lakes and coastlines along with the patterns of natural vegetation and the weather and climate. It is once you have this complete picture that you are then able to comprehend the historic events that have shaped the lives of the people and created the human landscapes with all their diversity.

We will look at the landscapes of the entire Mediterranean with regard to the mountain configuration, the valleys or plains, major rivers and islands. This will set the stage for the basic landscape of each of the ports of call.

THE MOUNTAINS: Although there is a similarity to the climatic patterns of the Mediterranean Sea, there are distinct local variations that are the result of which side of the sea the land is located, its variations in elevation and its exposure to inflowing moist or dry air. But so much of the variation in landscapes is determined by the mountain configuration of the region. Mountains tend to act as catchments for inflowing moisture and they also tend to serve as barriers. You have heard the terms windward and leeward used by mariners and by meteorologists. These terms refer to how mountains stand relative to the inflow of moist air. The struck side of a mountain range is the windward side, often wet and lush with vegetation while the opposing side receives far less rainfall or snowpack and is called the leeward slope.

When you look at a relief map of the Mediterranean Sea and the lands surrounding it, you will notice for the most part that the lands are mountainous, especially in Europe and Asia Minor. In North Africa there tends to be more level land fronting on the Mediterranean Sea, especially in Libya and Egypt.

* Iberian Peninsula - The peninsula that is home to Portugal and Spain is primarily dominated over by a moderately high central plateau in Spain often given the generic name of the Meseta. Within the plateau, several mountain ranges interrupt the otherwise gently rolling landscape. Along the western, southern and eastern margins of the Meseta the landscape is crumpled, warped or uplifted to produce numerous distinctive mountains. The most notable range of mountains is the venerable Sierra Nevada located just north of the Mediterranean Sea in the province of Andalucía. The highest peak reaches a maximum elevation of 11,418 feet (3,478 meters). These mountains are forested in pine and their high peaks are snow covered for over six months

out of the year. Many of the mountains in the Meseta or bordering it rise up to over 8,000 feet (2,400 meters) in height and are impressive in their own right.

* The Alpine System - From the Atlantic Ocean to the Adriatic Sea and beyond, the Alpine Mountain System dominates the landscape, essentially creating a distinct boundary zone between the Mediterranean and the cooler, more gentle landscapes of Central Europe. There are several components to the Alpine System, as noted below:
** Pyrenees Mountains - Forming a distinct border between Spain and France, the Pyrenees reach altitudes as high as 11,168 feet (3,404 meters). They are a relatively formidable barrier and have few pass routes. The Pyrenees are beautiful and many parts are thickly forested.
** The Alps - This is the highest and most famous core of the entire system, starting in southeastern France and extending along the northern border of Italy and Switzerland, Italy and Austria and Slovenia and Austria. Their highest elevation is 15,780 feet (4,810 meters) and there are many peaks over 12,000 feet (3,800 meters). The pass routes are narrow and road and rail lines must twist and turn to negotiate them. The Alps served to protect the core of the Roman Empire from invasions for centuries, and today they still inhibit movement between Italy and its neighbors to the north. The Alps are majestic, having been heavily glaciated, which left many peaks standing almost vertical against the sky, separated by deep valleys that once were packed with tons of ice scouring their way to sea level. No range of mountains anywhere in the world is as greatly loved by visitors as the Alps.
** The Carpathians - Extending in a northeasterly arc away from the Alps are the Carpathians, a less dominating range that runs through the Czech Republic and Slovakia into the Ukraine and Moldova. These mountains only reach a maximum elevation of 8,711 feet (2,655 meters), but they are beautifully forested and do provide recreation potential for the people of east central Europe. Essentially these mountains are well north of the Mediterranean Sea and not part of the region.
** Transylvanian Alps - The Carpathians merge into the Transylvanian Alps that curve in a wide arc back to the south, but do not reach the Mediterranean Sea. Some geologists refer to the Transylvanian Alps as the Southern Carpathians. They are a seldom-visited mountain range where remoteness has still left the traditional Romanian villages free of much outside influence. Their maximum elevation reaches a height of 8,346 feet (2,544 meters), but having been subjected to glacial action, they possess numerous sharp peaks and are quite majestic.

* The Apennine Mountains - This cordillera of several individual ranges runs the full length of the Italian Peninsula, serving as a rugged spine separating the two coasts of Italy. The Apennine are an ancient folded and up faulted

range still active from time to time, creating occasional severe earthquakes. Their maximum height is 7,103 feet (2,165 meters). They vary from gentle to rugged and do act as a distinct barrier through the middle of Italy.

* Standing apart from the Apennine Mountains are the two volcanic mountains of Mt. Vesuvius and the island volcano of Stromboli. The lie along a major zone that
is exceptionally active.

* The Balearic Islands, Corsica and Sardinia are the result of geologic uplift of a hard rock spine off the western coast of Italy. Both islands are exceptionally rugged, but their peaks only rise to a maximum elevation of 8,878 feet (3,350 meters) on the island of Corsica.

* Sicily - The largest island in the Mediterranean is Sicily, a very rugged island composed of several mountain ranges, and includes the large shield volcano of Mt. Etna with an elevation of 10,922 feet (3,329 meters), the most active volcanic peak in Europe.

* The Balkan Peninsula - Fronting on the eastern edge of the Adriatic Sea, the Balkan Peninsula is composed of numerous tightly packed mountain ranges that combine to produce an exceptionally rugged landscape, one also prone to periodic severe earthquakes, as this region is still geologically quite active. Despite their very rugged appearance, the mountains of the Balkan Peninsula reach a maximum elevation of only 9,596 feet (2,925 meters). There are many heavily forested areas that serve as recreational reserves, but much of the landscape has been put to human use and is dotted with villages and towns. The southern margin of the Balkan Peninsula is broken into numerous smaller peninsulas and then extends into the Aegean Sea in the form of hundreds of islands, primarily within Greece where they have become lionized by tourists for their mild climate and peaceful waters. Winter in the interior of the Balkans can be quite severe with heavy snows. Remember that the Bosnian city of Sarajevo hosted the winter Olympic games in 1984.

* Anatolia - The heart of Turkey is a great high altitude plateau called Anatolia, It is bounded by mountain rims that face outward toward the Aegean Sea and the far eastern Mediterranean Sea. There are numerous individual ranges, but the highest peaks known as the Taurus Mountains facing the sea that rise to a maximum elevation of 12,323 feet (3,086 meters) just west of the city of Antalya. They are spectacular and their snow-capped peaks can be seen well out to sea.

* The Levant - A series of parallel mountain ranges extend south from Anatolia and run through western Syria, Lebanon and Israel. These ancient mountains straddle a plate boundary between the Arabian and African Plates where a deep gash is found extending from the Sea of Galilee through the Dead Sea into the Red Sea. This is a volatile zone of infrequent, but catastrophic earthquakes. The mountains to the west do rise to significant heights of 10,131 feet (3,088 meters) in Lebanon. The rift zone dips to 1,407 feet (308 meters) below sea level, making this the lowest spot on earth. During winter, snow can cover most of the mountains of the Levant, a sight that most visitors would find strange since the landscape is rather barren, but most of the aridity is the result of the overgrazing of livestock over millennia.

* Island of Cyprus - This is an uplifted island that contains one mountain mass at its central core and a smaller fringe of mountain along its northern coast. The land reaches a maximum elevation of 6,404 feet (1,952 meters), much of the island being composed of high, rugged hills rather than mountains.

* Atlas Mountains - There is a great arc of mountains that begins in southern Morocco and extends northward to the Mediterranean and then runs east through Algeria into Tunisia where it comes to an end. This is one of only two major ranges of mountains on the African continent, but it is both the longest and highest. The Atlas are formidable mountains with their maximum peak reaching an impressive 13,671 feet (4,167 meters) in Morocco. The Atlas present a magnificent snow-capped vision seen from the lower coastal mountains of Morocco or from the Sahara Desert to the east. When cold fronts sweep across the Atlas, it can snow right down to the Mediterranean coast of Algeria and Tunisia on rare occasions. Unlike the mountains in Europe and Asia Minor, the Atlas are almost devoid of forest vegetation because of a combination of a drier climate and also serious overgrazing of sheep and goats for the last few thousand years.

THE DESERTS: In North Africa, the great Sahara Desert extends north into southern Tunisia, coastal Libya and Egypt. Here the land is relatively flat, covered with tracts of sand or gravel and devoid of most forms of vegetation other than clumps of dry grass and a few scattered shrubs. This is one of the driest and most desolate desert areas in the world, and it offers little to those who are seeking beautiful landscapes. However, there is a certain fascination to this bare landscape and given time, it can grow on you, but few have the opportunity to see it.

The desert of the Sinai Peninsula is exceptionally rugged with an outcrop of bare mountains jutting into the Red Sea. However, along the Mediterranean coast the Sinai is nothing more than a flat desert plain covered in reddish brown sand and gravel. In southern Israel it is called the Negev Desert, and along the shores of the Dead Sea there are several rocky outcrops in the form of large mesas that are also devoid of vegetation except in narrow canyons where there are a few springs that seep out because of the unconsolidated sub strata along the Great Rift Valley.

RIVERS: Several important rivers do flow into the Mediterranean Sea, and they are important to settlement, as they provide for a steady supply of water for irrigation and domestic use. Many important towns and cities have developed along these rivers; some where the rivers meet the sea.

Starting in southern Portugal and looking at the Mediterranean Sea we will explore those major rivers, moving in a clockwise manner all the way across Europe into Asia Minor and then across North Africa to the Atlantic Coast. The important rivers are:
* Tagus River - Flowing out of the Portuguese-Spanish border, the Tagus River opens into a broad estuary, forming a natural harbor for the great Portuguese city of Lisbon.

* Rhône River - This is one of Europe's major rivers, leaving Lake Geneva in Switzerland and flowing through a broad valley south to the Mediterranean and emptying through an extensive delta just west of the city of Marseille.
* Arno River - This is one of the most important rivers of northern Italy, flowing through the great renaissance city of Florence and emptying into the Tyrrhenian Sea north of Livorno.

* Tiber River - This relatively short river flows through the ancient city of Rome and has been so important in the history of the Roman Empire as well as modern Italy.

* Po River - This is the most important river in Italy. It rises in the Alps near the French border and flows east across the northern extent of the country, emptying into the great lagoon in which the city of Venice is located.

* Nile River is the longest river on earth. It rises out of the great lakes of the African Rift Valley along the Equator, the White and Blue Nile Rivers flow north, joining at Khartoum, Sudan, bringing life to an otherwise hostile land. There is an important saying that states, "The Nile is Egypt and Egypt is the Nile." For thousands of years, great civilization flourished along its banks, and today Egypt still depends upon this mighty river. The vast delta extends into the Mediterranean Sea, having been built over thousands of years by the periodic floods.

SUMMARY: You can see that the lay of the lands surrounding the Mediterranean is quite complex. Geographers find this one of the most challenging of regions to study because there is so much variety in the nature of the mountains, plateaus, plains and river systems let alone the complexity of the vegetation biomes. As a potential visitor, all you need to remember is that you will be in a very scenic and majestic part of the world where land and water intertwine to create landscapes that have enchanted painters and photographers and continue to do so today.

MAJOR PORTS OF CALL IN FRANCE

France is one of the larger countries of Western Europe both in land area and population. The country occupies 248,600 square miles (643,801 square kilometers) making it the size of the U. S. state of Texas. The population of 64,406,000 is relatively stable, as France has a low birth rate because of its high level of technology and cost of living. The diversity of the landscape gives France many local environments that vary from a rather blustery and cold maritime climate in the northwest to the high mountains of the French Alps to the mild and subtropical Mediterranean coast.

France is historically an ancient country, first having been brought under the Roman Empire, later becoming the core of the Holy Roman Empire. The country became unified as a single nation in 486 AD, going through a long history of kings, many of them despotic. The Republic of France emerged after the French Revolution in 1792. The history of France would fill the pages of a large text, and other than this basic information, would serve no practical purpose since the port visits are to what has always been a remote area of the country when it comes to the socio political aspects of its development.

Most people who think of the Mediterranean with regard to France immediately conjure up images of elegant villas with red tile roofs clinging to hillsides overlooking the blue sea in such places as Nice, Cannes and St. Tropez. And essentially they are correct, as the French Riviera has become synonymous with the entire Mediterranean coastline of southern Europe. If only that were the case. Actually the French Riviera is not that extensive, extending for approximately 100 miles (150 kilometers) from St. Tropez in the west to the border of the Principality of Monaco in the east. But many people equate Monaco with France since the two are physically and economically intertwined.

Most cruise ships that stop along the French Riviera usually will dock in Monaco, or possibly in Nice. And a very few dock in Marseille, which is essentially an industrial port city, but gateway to the interior agricultural region of Provence, one of the most beautiful regions in the country. This chapter will treat the three port cities of Marseille, Nice and St. Tropez, as these are where ships dock when visiting the southern French coast.

MARSEILLE:
This is the largest city on the French Mediterranean coast with a population of 1,560,000 residents, making it the second largest city in France. It is closely linked to Paris by express motorway, high-speed

railway and numerous flights. The city has been the country's gateway to the Mediterranean since the time of the ancient Greek and Roman worlds. With the Suez Canal, it is the major southern port for France. And with the close ties to its former North African colonies of Algeria and Tunisia, there has been a large Arab and Berber population living in Marseille for centuries.

Marseille has always had the reputation of being a port city with all that entails such as bars, brothels and a somewhat "scruffy" appearance combined with an equally rowdy core of dockworkers and seamen. To some degree that still holds true in the port area, but Marseille has outgrown that image that dates back to the days of sailing ships. Today Marseille is known for its high-tech sector that has transformed it from an industrial city to one of well educated highly paid workers. And with this change have come upmarket residential neighborhoods, shopping and cultural activities.

Not that many cruise itineraries include Marseille, as there is still an underlying belief that it offers little for the visitor. And most ships that do include it on their Mediterranean itineraries do so to enable guests to visit the villages and rural landscape of Provence, which is so much a part of French gastronomy and fine art.

Here are my recommendations for what to do when visiting Marseille if it is on your itinerary. You can accomplish a visit either by choosing one of the tours within the city or out into Provence offered by your cruise line or you can request a private car with a driver/guide at a higher cost. The second option enables you to see exactly those sights that would be of interest to you and within a time frame of your choosing. I personally prefer the private option, as I like to have time to explore the types of sights that are of value to me without being given a set timetable of stops, which is what you get on an organized tour. I also feel the private option is best for anyone who is interested in photography, as it enables you to stop where you want, something not possible on a coach tour. But remember the cost will be significantly higher unless you join forces with another individual or couple and split the cost. Then it will just about equal what a coach tour would cost. The third option is to strike out on your own, which I do not recommend unless you are comfortable with the French language and have a spirit of adventure. On your own you can use the city's extensive tram network and its Metro, but you will be spending a lot of time getting from one venue to the next. If you have visited Marseille before, then yes, this is an economical and enjoyable way to explore the city.

In and around Marseille, these are the must see sights:
* Old Port of Marseille - This is where the city's history from the middle ages and through the renaissance took place. And surrounding the Old Port is the

mixture of early architectural styles that represent the growth of Marseille. The best way to enjoy the old port is on foot once you are there.
* **Basillique Notre Dame de la Garde** - At Rue Fort-du-Sanctuaire, this is a grand structure dating originally to 1214. By the 16th century, the church had become a hilltop fortress and then the current main basilica was started in 1851. The view from the basilica on a clear day makes this a worthy stop.
* **Abbaye Saint Victor** - Located near the old port at #3 rue de l'Abbaye, this ancient church has been at the heart of Christianity in Marseille since the faith first came to the shores of France. The crypts under the church date back as far as the early Greek and Roman era.
* **Fort Saint-Jean** - Located in the Old Port, this fort dates to the 17th century, but it is built upon the foundation of the earlier one started in the 12th century. It has been charged with guarding the entrance to the Old Port and is filled with much of the historic ambiance of the city's past.
* **Musee des Civilisacions de l'Europe et de la Mediterranee** - Located at #1 Esplanade du J4, this is a unique museum that should be a must because it compares and contrasts all of the present day cultures and countries that front on the Mediterranean Sea. The building itself is 21st century, and this museum is unique in that it is totally contemporary in its exhibits.
* **Musee d'Historie de Marseille** - At Square Belsunce - Centre Bourse, this museum chronicles the long and complex history of the city of Marseille.
* **Corniche** - This is the seaside boulevard lined with shops, hotels and apartments facing the coastal beaches of Marseille, what is the considered one of the more beautiful parts of the city.

For those who are going on a tour of Provence, I will not make recommendations because there is so much to see in this vast region that it would be impossible to cover more than one or two venues in a day. Most people visiting Provence spend time in the city of Aix en Provence, which is the historic and cultural center of the region. Then there are the ancient hilltop towns that are part of the beauty and charm of the landscape. But I would need an entire book to detail all that there is to see, so suffice it to say that if you take one of the ship tours, you will be given the best possible cross section of the region in the short time allowed. If you do a private tour, then definitely visit Aix en Provence and simply enjoy the local countryside. But be sure and have your driver/guide suggest somewhere traditional for lunch.

DINING OUT: Marseille is a very large city, and there are many areas around the main harbor that can be a bit "gritty," but still colorful. It will be difficult to try and find some of the best restaurants that are well out of the central city. Thus I have indicated three good restaurants that are open for lunch and that are easy to reach either by ship's shuttle bus or by taxi from the harbor area. It is too far for most to walk to the central city.

* O'Bidul - This is one of the most popular restaurants for lunch not only for visitors but for locals as well. Open from noon to 2 PM, it is located at 79 rue de la Palud in the heart of the central city. The food is typically French and the service is excellent. You will find a diverse menu including seafood, poultry and meat dishes. Everything is fresh and beautifully prepared. You will not be disappointed. And the prices are moderate by French standards.
* Chez Ida - This is a superb restaurant just on the eastern edge of the heart of the city, located at 7 rue Ferdinand Rey. The restaurant offers excellent food and the ambiance is definitely a plus, with music that speaks to the soul of France. It is open from noon to 2 PM, and I would class its food as having a true flavor of Marseille
* La Table du Fort - This very excellent restaurant is located at 8 rue Fort Notre Dame and serves lunch between noon and 2 PM. Although a bit expensive, the food and service along with the ambiance make it worth splurging a bit. You can choose a three course lunch with wine that will provide you with ample servings and not so to speak break the budget.

NICE:
The majority of cruise itineraries do not usually include Nice, but rather include a port of call at Monte Carlo in the Principality of Monaco. Nice is adjacent to Monte Carlo with the average travel time on the express motorway being about 20 minutes. The cruise lines that stop in Monte Carlo include in their coach tours one that will visit Nice for half a day or one that will visit Nice and one or more of the neighboring hilltop towns such as Èze or St. Paul de Vence. This entire region of southeastern France and Monaco is referred to as the Côte d'Azur, or the blue coast. It is the heart of the French Riviera

Nice dates to 350 BCE, having been founded by the Greeks. After the fall of Rome, Nice joined the Genoese League in the 8th century. During the middle ages, Nice participated in numerous wars, taking sides with the various kingdoms of the region. It was not until the Treaty of Turin in 1860 that Nice and its surroundings finally became a part of the French Republic. The role of tourism did not become a major focus of the economy until the 1950's, and today it is an important part of the overall economic picture.

Nice has a population of 343,000 residents, making it the fifth largest city in France. Many small villages also surround it where there are thousands of vacation homes and villas belonging to the upper income residents of many countries. And just to the west of Nice is the city of Cannes, which has developed its reputation as a wealthy vacation spot. Cannes is also famous for its summertime Cannes Film Festival, which is one of the biggest events in the motion picture industry.

If your cruise ship docks in Monte Carlo, there will no doubt be a tour to Nice with a continuation on to Cannes or to Saint Paul de Vence. You of course can also have a private car and driver/guide to take you to Nice or Cannes, or you can travel from Monaco by train, a travel time to Nice of 20 minutes and to Cannes approximately 45 minutes. If your cruise line does offer a stop in Nice, you will have several options open to you either by means of ship sponsored coach tours, private cars with driver/guides or by venturing off on your own. The three major activities include:

* Spending the day touring Nice, and there is much to see and do, as will be noted below.
* Taking a tour either by coach or private vehicle into the surrounding hill country to visit one or more of the famous medieval hill towns, the most famous being Saint Paul de Vence.
* Taking a tour either by coach or private vehicle to Cannes to enjoy this fabled city of the rich.
* Taking a tour either by coach, private vehicle or train to Monte Carlo if your ship will not be stopping in the Principality of Monaco.

When in Nice, here are my recommended highlights that should be seen, many of which will be included in ship sponsored coach tours:
* **Old Town Nice known as Viellie Ville** - This is one of the most sought after architectural districts in all of France. The pastel buildings with their shuttered windows festooned with colorful flowerpots have become a symbol of the greater region of Provence, and a source material for thousands of artists. The best way to appreciate the Old Town is on foot once you get there.
* **Promenade des Anglais** - This is the beautiful waterfront promenade that runs parallel to the famous beach of Nice and it is the site of the major hotels. Again this is to be best enjoyed on foot.
* **Castle Hill** - Located on the waterfront, this is the best view of Nice that is worth the effort of the steep walk. However, if you are not physically fit, I do not recommend this stop despite its great view.
* **Villa and Gardens of Ephrussi de Rothschild** - Located on Avenue Ephrussi in Colla Blanche just east of the center of Nice on a narrow, rocky peninsula, this is a breathtaking pink villa overlooking the sea that is filled with artistic treasures and surrounded by magnificent gardens. It took Baroness Beátrice Ephrussi de Rothschild seven years to complete.
* **Musee Nacional Marc Chagall** - Located at Avenue du Docteur Menard, this museum is devoted to the work of the famous modern artist Marc Chagall, beloved by many or looked upon as rather by absurd by some. His work may be controversial, but it is famous worldwide.

* Cathedrale Sainte-Reparate - At #3 Place Rossetti, this is the city's great cathedral and it is a beautiful example of impressive Baroque architecture. The cathedral is closed between Noon and 2 PM daily.
* Musee d'Arte et d'Historie Palais Massena - Located in the heart of Nice at #65 rue de France, this is a major place for those interested in the long history of Nice. The museum also has outstanding beautiful grounds open for you to explore.

There are many interesting sights to be seen outside the city of Nice, but of course more than one can visit in a single day. I am recommending the most important sights grouped first around Èze and Saint Paul de Vence and then around Cannes to make it easier to reference:
* Saint Paul de Vence - Located about 30 minutes north of Nice, this medieval hilltop town is one of the most beautiful in all of France. It is an architectural masterpiece with its narrow streets and crowded buildings serving as a hilltop crown. The entire village is created out of stone and appears to fit naturally into the landscape. It offers superb views from its northeastern terrace and on a clear day you can see the French Alps. The Hotel Saint Paul has a Michelin Star restaurant and if you want a truly grand lunch, but an expensive one, book ahead if you traveling privately. Some ship tours to Saint Paul de Vence will include lunch at the hotel.
* La Jardin exotique d"Èze - Located in the beautiful town of Èze overlooking the sea, this tropical garden set atop a hill is a magnificent sight.
* Vieux Èze - This is the old stone village at the center of Èze that offers a wonderful example of the ancient styles of architecture of southeastern France.
* Rue de Antibes - This is the most expensive and elegant shopping street in Cannes, a place where millionaires and movie celebrities rub shoulders with ordinary tourists who come to window shop. But it exemplifies the extravagance that Cannes is known for.
* Monastere de Cimiez - Located on Place Jean Paul II in the heart of Cannes, this monastery is home to many magnificent frescoes that are quite precious. The monastery also has excellent gardens.
* Le Suzuet - This is the hillside Old Town district of Cannes that offers cobbled streets, pastel houses and great views over the entire city from the top of the hillside. The Old Town is best seen on foot.
* Rue Meynadier - One of the most beautiful streets in the historic Old Town of Cannes, this is a place to savor, stop and have a coffee or aperitif in one of its cafes and just soak in the flavor of the city.
* Foyville Market - At #12 Rue Louis Blanc in Cannes, this is one of the best lessons in the freshness and variety of produce, cheeses and meats that go into the famous gastronomy of Provence

DINING OUT: Nice is a relatively large and spread out city and unless your cruise ship docks here, getting around on foot after traveling by train or motor coach from either Marseille or Monte Carlo is rather difficult. Thus I am only recommending three restaurants that are centrally located.

* Pastry Plaisirs - Located at 11 rue Delille in central Nice, it is a delightful place for both a typical French lunch menu and also for its delectable pastries. After all this is France, and pastry is an art in this country. The restaurant serves only lunch and is open from noon to 3 PM daily.

* Les Sens - Located at 37 Rue Pastorelli in central Nice is only open between noon and 2 PM for lunch, but does re open at 7:30 PM for dinner. This is a relatively expensive traditional French restaurant serving absolutely exquisite meals accompanied by fine wines. A reservation would be a must just to insure a table. If you want to partake of an extensive and superb menu, this is the place.

* Le Sejour - Located at 11 rue Grimaldi in central Nice, this is a delightful restaurant for lunch. It has an extensive menu and accompanying wine list and is open both for breakfast and lunch from very early morning until 2 PM. The food and service are both superb, and fresh fish and seafood figure prominently on their menu.

SAINT TROPEZ:
Located 62 miles (100 kilometers) west of Nice, Saint Tropez is truly the home of the rich and famous who are looking for seclusion and an escape from the night life and "glitz" of Nice or Cannes. It is essentially a village with less than 6,000 full time residents. Saint Tropez dates back to Roman times when it was the site of beautiful seaside villas. After the fall of Rome, it became home to many Saracen Muslims in the 9th century. One of the most unique visits occurred in 1516 when a group of Japanese Samurai were on their way to Rome, but were forced to land due to a storm. It is believed to be the first contact between Japan and Europe.

The 20th century many of France's fashion designers like Coco Chanel discovered Saint Tropez, and this began its rise to fame as a getaway resort for the rich and famous. But during World War II, it languished. When the Allied forces first landed in southern France, it was at Saint Tropez/

Today the town still retains its central core flavor as an old French fishing village, however, there is little fishing done. Rather it is filled with restaurants and boutiques catering to the throngs of visitors. All around the old town are the secluded villas that are hard to see because of the walls and thick vegetation affording the owners privacy.

Many visitors come in their own sailboats or yachts, and the marina is filled to capacity with the most expensive of watercraft. There is a small airport located about 9 miles (15 kilometers) outside of town. No rail service is provided, and the best way to come is by road, boat or cruise ship. But even cruise ships cannot anchor and must tender their guests ashore.

WHAT TO SEE IN SAINT TROPEZ: This is essentially a small village, but one with a million dollar plus price tag. The old center of town is relatively small, but today most of the old buildings house fine quality boutiques, cafes and bars. There is quite a bit of activity on the main street both during the day and evening, as visitors come to party and enjoy the ambiance.

There are a few sights of note, but for the most part this is a beach resort and not the type of place people come for major sightseeing. The few important venues are:

* **Citadelle de Saint-Tropez** - This was once the most major fortress along the coast, protecting French interests against pirates and foreign navies. The ramparts and buildings average over 400 years in age, but the highlight is the new Musée Naval de la Citadelle that is housed within once grim dungeon of the main citadel building. It is open from 10 AM to 6:30 PM daily, and worthy of at least one hour or more of your time. It is an easy walk from the center of town up to the citadel.

* **Eigles Notre-Dame de l'Assomption** - This is the main church whose steeple dominates over the town center. The church is old, some visitors say it is crumbling, but keep in mind it has been there for centuries and is an historic landmark. Yet it is in no way a grand building, just historic.

* **Plage de Pampelonne** - This is the beautiful beach that lies just south of the town center, a distance a bit too far to walk on your own. The water is crystal clear and the beach is very clean, but if traveling with children or teens, you may wish to watch out for those areas where people sun themselves partially nude. There are delightful cafes along the beachfront, as this is the place to take the sun and be seen.

* **Place de Lices Market** - Located in the center of town at Place des Lices. This is supposed to be a diverse marketplace, but clothing seems to dominate over food products. It is popular with day trippers such as cruise ship visitors, but most people who know Saint Tropez consider it over rated and the merchants less than friendly. I only mention it because of its popularity, but frankly state that ten minutes is about all you want to stay unless you are really into this type of shopping.

This may be a very small list, but there are no other historic monuments of note in Saint Tropez. You may wish to avail yourself of one of your ship tours if it is going to drive along the coast and visit any of the other beach resorts.

But simply by coming on shore and walking around, you will not be overly impressed.

SHOPPING: Yes for those who love to shop at high-end stores, Saint Tropez is the kind of upmarket village you will enjoy. Here is the only unique listing, keeping away from the recognized name brand stores:
* **La Maison des Confitures** - You will need a taxi to get here, but if you are into fine quality jams, jellies and marmalades, you must visit. Located along Route du Bourrian in the village of Gassin, it is about 15 minutes by taxi from the town center. Open from 9:30 AM to 8 PM, you will no doubt buy something while here.

DINING OUT: While in Saint Tropez, you no doubt will want to have a nice lunch, but be prepared for high prices. There are few restaurants among the better quality choices that are open for lunch. Most confine their hours strictly to dinner. And the majority of restaurants are located outside of the center of Saint Tropez where you will need transportation. But here are two good choices:
* **Restaurant le G'** - Located in town at 67 Rue du Portal Neuf and open from Noon to Midnight, this is a good place for lunch. The food, service and ambiance are what you would expect in Saint Tropez and it always receives primarily high ratings from guests. Plan on at least 30 to 40 Euro per person for a three-course lunch.
* **Le Dit Vin** - In the center of town at 7 Rue de la Citadelle and open from 11:30 AM until well past Midnight, this is a delightful restaurant with a primarily organic menu. The flavors are those of the Mediterranean style of cooking, fresh and light served with accompanying wines. They also have a late afternoon and evening tapas bar.

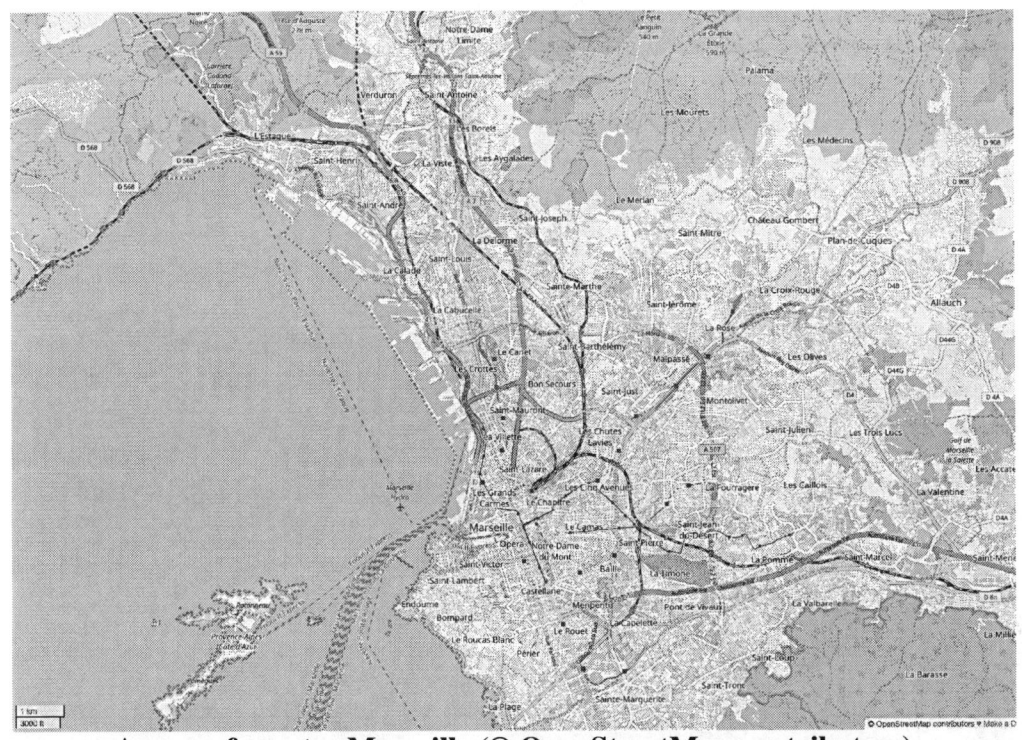

A map of greater Marseille (© OpenStreetMap contributors)

Looking down on Marseille with a view to the north

In the Old Town harbor of Marseille (Work of Thomas Steiner, CC BY SA 3.0, Wikimedia.org)

Fausse Monnaie Bridge leading to Endoume, (Work of TouNCC BY SA 3.0, Wikimedia.org)

The main port of Nice (Work of Alistair Cunningham, CC BY SA 3.0, Wikimedia.org)

In the main public square of Nice

A traditional street with shuttered buildings in the old core of Nice

There is a definite flavor in Nice that speaks to Provence

The old medieval hill town of Èze close to the Monaco border

The old hill town of Saint Paul de Vence

On the back streets of historic Saint Paul de Vence

The old village fountain in Saint Paul de Vence

An aerial view of Saint Tropez village

A hillside view over the village of Saint Tropez

Looking onshore to Saint Tropez and its Citadel hill

The more modern beach resorts across the bay from Saint Tropez

MAJOR PORT OF CALL IN GIBRALTAR

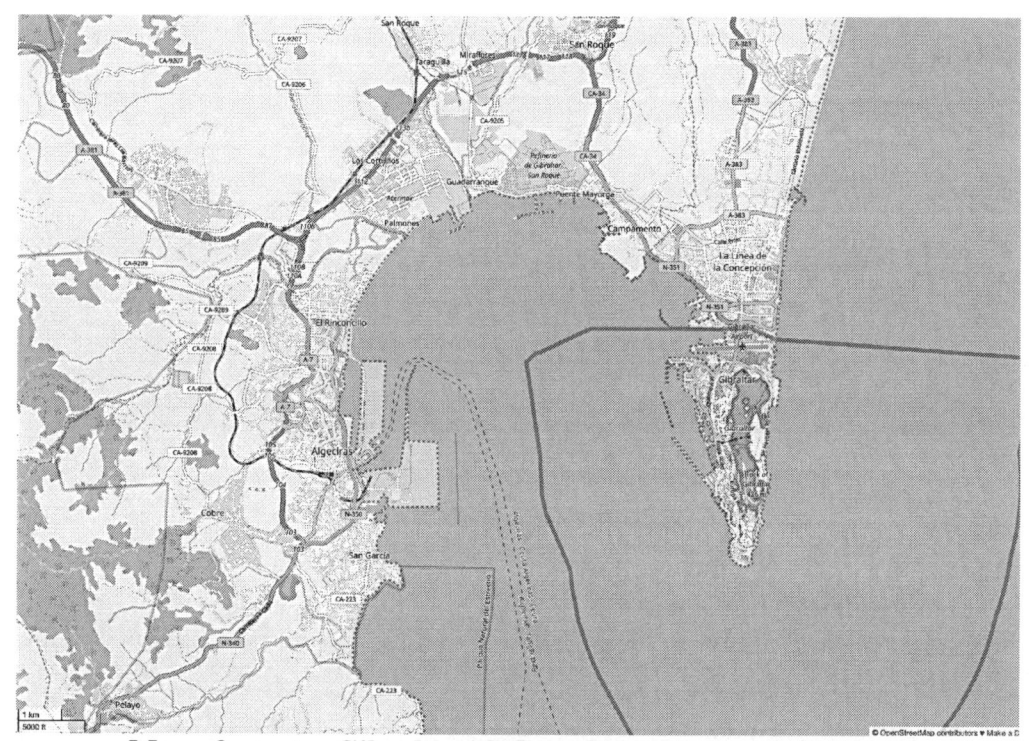

Map of greater Gibraltar (© OpenStreetMap contributors)

Gibraltar is an overseas territory of the United Kingdom. It is a very small parcel of land, occupying only 6.8 square kilometers (2.6 square miles). The resident population is 32,200, primarily a mix of British, Spanish, Indian and Maghrebi with English, Spanish and Ladino the three primary languages. The people do have a major degree of home rule, but there is an appointed governor who represents the crown. The official head of state is Her Majesty, Queen Elizabeth II.

Because of the territory being so small and having its only land boundary with Spain, traffic now flows on the right rather than on the left.

The Rock of Gibraltar is such a dominant landform feature in an area of lower hills and coastal plains that it always afforded a commanding view and ultimately a measure of control over the narrowing width of the far western Mediterranean Sea that it was considered to be of strategic value. The rock is composed of limestone from the Jurassic Age, dating back over 70 million years ago. It is essentially a monolith, meaning it is a solitary rock formation rising up 428 meters, or 1,398 feet above the sea. Being composed of limestone, it erodes easily under the influence of water and thus the rock is honeycombed with natural caves, which have made it easier to develop a string of defensive artillery positions within the rock. The British fully developed the strategic value and made it virtually impossible for an invasion force to capture Gibraltar.

Across the Mediterranean in Morocco is its counterpart known as Jebel Musa, but geologically its origin is different. Standing at 841 meters or 2,762 feet above the sea, it is much higher and wider than Gibraltar. Together they make up the mythological Pillars of Hercules, which in ancient Greek and Roman times marked the western edge of the known world, as beyond lay lands and seas uncharted by mariners of the day. According to Greek myth, Hercules had to split the barrier blocking in the Mediterranean Sea, thus creating the two pillars. But Jebel Musa is part of a chain of mountains called the Rif that runs east to west across northern Morocco and then picks up across the narrow opening to the Mediterranean and sweeps across southern Spain.

Even in today's world, entering or leaving the Mediterranean Sea by way of the Straits of Gibraltar makes one wonder about all the ancient Greek mythology about this famous body of water. And the most puzzling story of all is that of Atlantis, which Plato said was to be found beyond the Straits of Gibraltar. Some speculate that the Azores, Madeira or the Canary Islands are all candidates, where most now support the belief that Atlantis was the current Greek island of Santorini in the Aegean Sea, well in the opposite direction from Gibraltar. But in any event, passing through the straits with or without a stop in Gibraltar gives one the opportunity to look at Europe and Africa at the same time.

WHAT TO SEE OR DO IN GIBRALTAR: The territory of Gibraltar is very tiny, but the rock dominates most of the land, leaving only a fringe that is settled. Streets are narrow and many rise steeply up the lower sides of the cliff. To enjoy a view from the top requires a climb on foot that is simply too steep and difficult for the majority of cruise passengers, especially during periods of warmest weather. Thus my recommendation is for every ship passenger going ashore in Gibraltar to take one of the ship's sponsored coach tours. In this way you have the services of a guide and the coach to negotiate the terrain. Normally I prefer a private car and driver/guide, but frankly in Gibraltar it is not worth the cost simply because the distances are so minimal and there is not that much of great significance to see.

The most important sights for visitors not to miss in Gibraltar are:
* The Rock of Gibraltar - Without doubt the rock is the major attraction. All coach tours feature the rock, some more extensive than others. The most thrilling part of visiting the rock is to experience the drive to the top and then

to marvel at the incredible view of two continents. You look out to the north across the Spanish countryside and then turn around and look across to the shores of Morocco in Africa just a few kilometers distance. Inhabiting the rock is a troupe of Barbary Apes, actually they are macaques, and very "cheeky." They will steal anything that you do not have a tight grip on, especially food items. Many visitors bring bananas for the monkeys. And often it creates a bit of havoc, as they vie for the offerings.

You can reach the top of the rock on the major ship tours, by taxi or you can also ride the dramatic cable car. From the gondola on a clear day you get a dramatic ascending and descending view and also see the face of the rock close up.

There are natural limestone caves at the lower levels of the rock and then the man made tunnels and gun emplacements that are included on most tours, which are especially impressive. Of the lower caves, Saint Michael's Cave is the most spectacular, this being a geological sight of great beauty. Normally you can spend two to three hours on the rock to see all the major sights, which is well worth the time spent.

* Mediterranean Steps - I am reluctant to recommend this very popular attraction among those who are young and fit. If you want to truly appreciate the magnitude of the Rock of Gibraltar and if you are absolutely in great physical shape, then this is the way to the top for the stunning views offered. But under no circumstances attempt this walk if you are not in excellent shape.

* Grand Casemates Square - This is the major public square of Gibraltar and it definitely has a distinctive flavor. The architecture is more typically Spanish even though this is a British Colony. Historically this was once a military parade ground surrounded by barracks. Today it is a public square surrounded by restaurants and souvenir stores. It is also the start of the city's main street.

* Main Street - Leading off Grand Casemates Square, this is a pedestrian street that is the commercial heart of Gibraltar. You will find a mix of locals and tourists and the shops also are a mix of those serving local need and those devoted to visitors. What visitors like is the fact that shopping for major purchases does offer the advantages of being duty free.

* Gibraltar Museum - At 18/20 Bomb House Lane in the center of town, this small museum does have a good array of exhibits and artifacts covering the colonial history.

* Europa Point - This is said to be the most southerly point in Europe, clearly the southern tip of the Gibraltar Peninsula. The ground level views out over the coastline and the view across to Morocco are very striking. There are public facilities and a cafe, making this a popular stop. But geographically,

Malta is considered to still be a part of Europe, and it is actually farther south. Thus Europa Point is the southernmost piece of continental Europe.

* Moorish Castle - Located on the lower margin of the rock, this somewhat crumbling castle does remind you of the important Moorish role played in the history of southern Spain. It was the Moors who invaded from Africa and ruled most of Spain for centuries until ejected by King Ferdinand and Queen Isabella in the late 15th century. The castle, once a major fortification, does offer some great lower level views of the city and the rock behind.

SHOPPING TIPS: There are few specific craft items native to the area, most everything by way of craft being Spanish in origin, or brought over from Morocco. Shopping simply means duty free. There is really nothing you could buy in Gibraltar that you could not buy at home. The only difference is the savings on the import duty.

I have no specific shops to recommend because I do not find this a port of call where shopping is a major factor other than to save some money on more luxury-oriented items.

DINING OUT: The majority of fine restaurants are not open for lunch, and most ship itineraries have you leaving before dinner hour. The types of cuisine found in Gibraltar will be relatively variable, but Spanish and North African dishes are the ones that represent the area you are in. I have selected a few dining establishments that are open for lunch and do offer the flavors of the region. My choices are:

* The Lounge Gastro Bar - Located in the Marina at 17 Ragged Staff Wharf off the Queensway Quay, this restaurant offers fresh food, friendly and efficient waiters and a nice atmosphere facing the water. The menu is more contemporary and international, but the main key is the fact that everything is made in house and is of high quality.

* Gauchos - Located on Fishmarket Street just outside of Casemates Square, this is a place to come for meat. Beef and lamb are the specialties, and in true Spanish or Argentine fashion, it is grilled the way you like it because you are given super hot stones on which to finish off your preparation.

* Cafe Rojo - Located in Irish Town, this is an excellent restaurant featuring the cuisine of the Mediterranean, including Spanish, French and Italian dishes. Everything is done to perfection and this is a gem of a restaurant.

FINAL NOTE: Most readers of this book will not get to visit Gibraltar because only a handful of itineraries include the port. But if you are sailing by during daylight hours, you will be able to see the famous Rock of Gibraltar and with binoculars, you can at least get the feel of almost having been there.

The Rock of Gibraltar seen from across the border in Spain (Work of InfoGibraltar, CC BY SA 2.0 Wikimedia.org)

Looking down on Gibraltar Port from the Rock (Work of Bengt Nyman, CC BY SA 3.0, Wikimedia.org)

The Old Town Square in Gibraltar

Main Street in Gibraltar (Work of Olaf Tausch, CC BY SA 3.0, Wikimedia.org)

Another view of Main Street, Gibraltar

Night in quaint Irish Town (Woprk of John Cummings, CC BY SA 3.0, Wikimedia.org)

MAJOR PORTS OF CALL IN MOROCCO

A map of Morocco that does not include Western Sahara, which Morocco claims as their territory

A visit to Morocco may be part of your cruise itinerary in the Western Mediterranean, either stopping for a day in the exotic port of Tangiers, or you may be on a cruise that left one of the Mediterranean ports such as Barcelona or Málaga and is traveling beyond the Mediterranean to the Island of Madeira or the Canary Islands with a stop in Casablanca. In either case, you will get a taste of North Africa at its finest, as Morocco is a country that ties together both the ancient Berber and later Arab cultures along with touches of European influence.

Morocco is the only country on the continent of Africa that touches both on the Atlantic Ocean and the Mediterranean Sea. It is a relatively large country, occupying 710,850 square kilometers or 274,460 square miles. And it has a total population of 33,848,000. This is a country where 99 percent of the people are a mix of Arab and Berber, with Sunni Islam being the official religion of the nation. Shia Islam, Judaism and Christianity are all recognized minority faiths.

Morocco is a constitutional monarchy, but one in which a significant amount of governing authority is still vested in the king. Currently His Majesty, Mohammed VI is the king of the nation, and he is well liked by his people.

The main distinguishing geographic feature of Morocco is the range of mountains that extends right across the length of the nation, including the northernmost Rif Mountains. The Atlas Mountains are the longest chain of mountains in Africa, and their tallest peak within Morocco reaches 4,167 meters or 13,671 feet. The Atlas are a formidable range, their snow covered peaks only penetrated by a few high pass routes. Although high and snow covered, there are few forests on the middle slopes of the Atlas, mankind long ago having stripped the land bare in reckless abandon. The Atlas form the divide between the milder coastal region of the country and the exceptionally dry interior.

Air blowing in off the Atlantic Ocean brings significant winter rainfall to the coastal mountains and valleys, giving Morocco a Mediterranean type climate that is very productive. And the orographic impact of the Atlas Mountains create major snowfields that provide melt water during the dry summer. Beyond the Atlas Mountains Morocco shares the westernmost edges of the Sahara Desert. Here vast fields of sand dunes and gravel-covered plains present an almost lifeless landscape. Towns on the lower western margins of the Atlas Mountains such as Fez and Marrakesh are famous as contact points where camel caravans from across the Sahara come to trade.

Morocco is an ancient land that has been inhabited for somewhere over 100,000 years, dating back to the Paleolithic or Old Stone Age. The only information on these early hunting-gathering civilizations is based upon the stone artifacts found by archaeologists.

By the time of Eastern Mediterranean historic recordkeeping, the Phoenicians are known to have been the first to trade along the coast of what is now Morocco around 600 BCE.

Ultimately Morocco was brought under the control of ancient Carthage (modern Tunisia), which was originally settled by Phoenicians. By 110 BCE, there was a native Berber kingdom established in what is now northern Morocco. By 100 BCE, northern Morocco was under Roman influence and by 200 AD, Christianity had been introduced into the few Roman settlements. By the 5th century, Rome's influence waned and the Vandals and Visigoths briefly had forays into the region. But by the 6th century, the Byzantine Empire from Constantinople had spread its influences. However, the majority of the Berber people living away from the coast were never drawn under the influence of these invading cultures.

It was not until after the year 670, that Islam began to make headway across North Africa, moving steadily westward through coastal communities. By the early 700's, there was an independent Berber Islamic state in the Rif Mountains, and after the Berber uprising of 739, other Berber Islamic states were founded.

Through the 8th and 9th centuries, there were several rises and falls of Berber states, the longest lasting was the Idrisids who established Fez in 788, and their power lasted until 927. But later Berber dynasties arose and ruled into parts of southern Spain and Portugal until the 13th century when Arab tribes migrated into what are now Algeria and Morocco, thus ending Berber power.

After the fall of the Moors in southern Spain, both Portuguese and Spanish explorations and colonial expansion made their influence felt along the Moroccan coast, but not into the stronghold of the Berber and Arabs who still ruled the interior. Ultimately the Arab dynasties consolidated their hold over much of what is now Morocco. By 1666, the Alaouite Dynasty had come to rule all of Morocco, and they still rule today. By 1700, there was no Spanish, Portuguese or British held territory on Moroccan soil. In 1786, Sultan Mohammed III gave protection to American merchant ships against the Barbary Pirates; this after Morocco was the first nation to extend diplomatic recognition to the United States in 1777. The treaty negotiated in 1786 still holds to the present.

During the 19th century, Spain, France and the British began to establish their footholds into North Africa. Spain had expanded its territory of Ceuta in 1860 on the Mediterranean and established a protectorate status over Morocco. France joined with Spain in 1904, creating their zones of protection. The British and German governments resented this move, and tensions built to where negotiations finally led to an easing of tensions with other territories in Africa having been carved up by the major powers. France created a Moroccan protectorate through negotiations with the king in 1912, but it left

Spain in control of its tiny enclaves, and its control over Spanish Sahara to the south of Morocco. Thousands of French colonists moved into Morocco, and their cultural and linguistic influences are still felt today. Working closely with the Moroccan government, France and Morocco successfully ran the country in a quasi-independent status.

What ultimately led to the full independence of Morocco was the 1953 exile of Sultan Mohammed V to Madagascar because of his opposition to French power. When France placed an unpopular puppet on the throne, this led to violence against Europeans in the country. King Mohammed V returned in 1955 and one year later Morocco gained its full independence. Spain also relinquished control of all but the two tiny Mediterranean enclaves of Ceuta and Melilla, which they still hold today.

The most notorious king of modern Morocco has been King Hassan II, as he initially encouraged free elections in 1961, then suspended parliament in 1965 after internal strife. In 1971, there was an attempt to depose the king, but it failed. A truth commission did, however, reveal much of the repressive activity of King Hassan II's rule.

However, in 1973, when King Hassan II asked for volunteers to enter Spanish Sahara to help in a movement to oust Spain, he did get over 350,000 volunteers. In the end, Spanish forces vacated, but Moroccan forces remained and along with Mauritania to the south, they divided the territory. Algeria sent in troops and there were clashes, but to the present day, Morocco lays claim to most of former Spanish Sahara. A United Nations ceasefire has essentially held, but Morocco still holds nominal control.

In 1999, King Mohammed VI came to the throne and he has slowly modernized the country and introduced more liberal laws. His internal policies have been more enlightened and he has strong popular support at home. However, the crisis in Western Sahara, formerly Spanish Sahara, remained unresolved. The United Nations was unable to broker any resolution. And there are still tensions between Spain and Morocco over the two Spanish enclaves.

Morocco has to date experienced three major incident of al-Qaeda inspired terrorism when 40 people or more were killed in a Casablanca bombing in 2003 of a Spanish restaurant and Jewish center. The perpetrators were given only ten-year sentences. In 2007, another Casablanca bombing fortunately injured only three people, but the government did hand down long prison sentences for the incident. In 2011, a bombing in Marrakesh killed 17 in a local cafe, again a splinter al-Qaida group claimed responsibility.

What seems to have quelled any further potential for violence has been a referendum to bring about major reforms at the request of the king. So far, many reforms have been introduced, but there are many more that have not yet been implemented, prompting the most recent demonstrations in 2012. It is hoped that Morocco can maintain its stability and not go the way of so many other Middle Eastern nations. What is fortunate is that the economy overall is quite strong with heavy agricultural exports, mining of phosphates, major fishing exports and the heavy role of tourism.

CASABLANCA:
There is no other city in the greater Mediterranean and North African region of the world with a name more recognized than Casablanca. And it is not because of the city, but rather the influence of Hollywood. The 1942 film starring Humphrey Bogart and Ingrid Bergman has become such an iconic classic that its name is even recognized by today's youth. Casablanca (the film) has helped put the city's name firmly into people's mind. And in the film, the now legendary Rick's Bar actually has its counterpart in the old sector of the city of Casablanca, complete with piano.

Although the largest city and great port for Morocco, Casablanca is not the national capital. The capital is located in Rabat, about one hour north of Casablanca by highway or rail. Casablanca is a large city with a metropolitan population of 4,270,000, but many estimate the population at being possibly as high as 6,000,000. I would rather err on the conservative side, as the city has never seemed that large despite its crowding and congested streets. Some travel writers have called it Morocco's ugliest city while others see through the congestion and the lack of an organized plan and find it a colorful and fascinating city. I tend to be in the latter camp. Casablanca is overwhelming to the uninitiated visitor, but it does give a good representation of North African urban life.

WHAT TO SEE AND DO: Given that for most first time visitors to Morocco, the city of Casablanca can be an overload to the senses, so I recommend that unless you are quite adventurous, you are better off taking one of the organized ship's tours or having the cruise line order a private car with a driver/guide. Unless you know exactly what you want to see, it is better to get a programmed overview of the city, learn about its history and be guided through its various districts. But if you are adventurous, you can take the ship's shuttle into the city center and then strike out on your own. But keep in mind that you are in a conservative Islamic country, and it could be very easy to say or do something that could cause you some difficulty. Thus at the very least, find a taxi driver with whom you can converse in English or French, and explain the types of sights you wish to see. Also ask the driver to accompany you when you leave the car on any stop where there are crowds, especially if you want to take a lot of pictures.

The most important sights to see are as follows:
* Hassan II Mosque - This is the number one attraction in Casablanca, and as your ship docks, you can see it on the skyline. This is the 7th largest mosque in the Islamic World. It sits on a cliff overlooking the Atlantic Ocean and has a massive courtyard in front. Tours are given during times where group prayers are not in progress, and definitely not on Friday afternoons. This is the only mosque in the city that offers tours, and other mosques do not permit non-believers to enter. You must take your shoes off to enter the mosque, and women's knees, heads and shoulders must be covered out of respect. The mosque was opened in 1993. The main minaret stands the height of a 60-story building, and it is the world's tallest. At night a laser light shines in the direction of Mecca. The building is constructed of marble and the decorations are all hand-carved, having taken thousands of hours to create. The interior can hold up to 25,000 worshipers.
* Old Medina - This is the old walled city with its crooked streets, narrow lanes and traditional adobe buildings. It can be daunting to visitors, and I recommend not visiting without a guide or taxi driver who can serve as an escort. There are well over 1,500 individual stalls that sell every imaginable product, and bargaining is expected. For a foreign visitor this is quintessential Morocco, but not to be experienced on your own.
* Place des Nations Unies- This is the heart of new Casablanca. It is in many ways like the downtown area of any big city, but it is worth a walk because despite being more modern, it still oozes a Moroccan flavor that foreigners will find it quite fascinating. The actual main street is Boulevard Mohammed V, which begins initially as a pedestrian and light rail only street and then widens into a major thoroughfare. In the middle is Mohammed V Square, one of the major hubs of the city center that is very colorful.
* Musee Abderrahman Slaoui - Located in the city center at 12 rue du Parc, this is the premier museum where you can see the culture and history of Morocco come alive. Quartier Habous - Located in the city center on Boulevard Victor Hugo, this old neighborhood has a great collection of buildings with typical traditional architecture. The district is also filled with a variety of craft and souvenir shops for those who also want to do some local shopping.
* Marche Central - Located on Boulevard Mohammed V at the Marche Central station on the light rail, this is a public market where you will see a great variety of fish, fresh vegetables and fruits and many traditionally prepared Moroccan dishes ready for people to take home. And if you are polite, you can get some samples to taste.

There are many more interesting venues around the city, but these will require that you be on a coach tour or have a private car or taxi. There are many neighborhoods of interest. In the southern part of the city you will find the more upscale districts with both beautiful residential streets and nice shopping centers. The northern part of the city is the lower income area that is quite crowded with many street bazaars. But it would be a mistake to try and visit this part of the city on your own without a guide or even a competent taxi driver, as you would be quite conspicuous as a tourist. However, if properly escorted, you will see a grittier side to life in Casablanca.

DINING OUT: Most visitors who come on a cruise that stops in Casablanca are often reluctant to go out sightseeing or dining on their own. The vast majority will see the city as part of an organized tour that may be half day or full day that would include lunch, but with no choice of restaurant or menu. For those who are more adventurous, I have three excellent recommendations, but I do suggest that you do not try and find these restaurants on your own. Either have the cruise line arrange a car and driver for your day or ask port security to call a reputable taxi to take you to sightseeing and to lunch. Do not attempt to hire a taxi without knowing anything about the company. Casablanca is relatively safe, but remember this is North Africa and you are a foreigner.

If you are out on your own in Casablanca, I do highly recommend that you try a traditional Moroccan lunch. The exotic nature of the way Moroccan cuisine is spiced is something to be remembered. The most common method of cooking is to roast meat and vegetables together with dried fruits in a clay pot with a tall chimney like lid. It is called a tagine, as are the wonderful dishes cooked within this unique pot. Meat generally served will include lamb or goat, sometimes beef or chicken. And in Casablanca there is an abundance of seafood. Rice pilaf or couscous will almost always be a part of the meal and among vegetables, eggplant, zucchini and carrots are commonplace. Depending upon the type of roast tagine you order there can also be dried prunes, apricots or dates to add sweetness to the dish.

Most of the top restaurants unfortunately are only open for dinner, but I have listed a few that do serve lunch in Moroccan style. Many cruise ships do stay until late in the evening if they have a group traveling to Marrakesh, but the dock area is difficult to negotiate at night, and you will not be able to find a taxi. The only way to have dinner out would be to have the shore concierge arrange a private car in advance.

These are my recommendations for a traditional Moroccan lunch, but please

note that these restaurants will not satisfy everyone, as the best restaurants are not available at lunch:
* Restaurant Cafe La SQALA - Located on Boulevard des Almohades near the Medina. It is best to take the shuttle bus to the city center and then hail a taxi unless you have a private car. Open from 8 AM to 11 PM, this fine Moroccan restaurant serves both indoors and in a beautiful courtyard. The food is traditional and it has one of the best overall ratings for the luncheon meal.
* Al Mounia - This traditional Moroccan restaurant is located in Liberte, what could be called downtown. It is at 95 rue du Prince Moulay-Abdallah and is open daily for lunch and dinner. Reservations would be recommended. This is a relatively expensive restaurant and the featured dishes are tajines, the very exotic meat, poultry or fish dish with elegant spices and usually served with couscous. This is a true Moroccan experience flavor wise, but it is designed for visitors.
* Rick's Cafe - Yes there is a Rick's in Casablanca, and it is in the old city just as you would expect. This is definitely tourist oriented and based upon the movie "Casablanca," but never existed in the time period of the movie. Lunch is served from noon to 3 PM, and the food is exceptionally good with true Moroccan flavor. So in this case who cares if it is a tourist oriented restaurant. It is fun, it is safe and best of all it is good.
* Zayna - Located at Place Habous, Rue ibn Khaldoune 44 in the Quartier Habous, and open from 10 AM to 11 PM. You will need to take a taxi from the shuttle drop off point, as it is too far to walk. This is one of the finest Moroccan restaurants and you will find the food to be tasty and well prepared. The restaurant and all of its facilities are spotlessly clean.

Despite its great size, Casablanca does not offer many restaurants at luncheon that most visitors out on their own will feel totally comfortable at, but these two I have listed are top notch.

SHOPPING: Morocco is a country noted for its traditional handcrafts. Hammered brassware and handmade carpets are among the most sought after traditional crafts. Both can be rather bulky items to pack, so it is important to shop with dealers who are reputable and will ship your treasures home.

This is my sole recommendation as to where to shop in Casablanca for traditional Moroccan crafts:
* Exposition Nationale d'Artisanat - This artist's market is located at 3 Avenue Hassan II not far from the Marche Central and easily reached from the Marche Central light rail stop. It has a mix of traditional crafts and souvenirs, so you need to be very careful with what you buy. And if possible, having a guide with you is a big help in the event you want to make a serious purchase.

FINAL NOTE: Many who visit Casablanca are pleased with the vibrant color and excitement of the city. Others find it somewhat less appealing. I have even heard some visitors say it is dirty, and that unfortunately is not true. Remember that Morocco is still primarily a third world country, but Casablanca is its crown jewel with regard to being the sophisticated national center of culture.

MARRAKESH:
If you really are interested in buying traditional Moroccan craft items or rugs, it is best to take a ship's all day tour to Marrakesh, which is the most celebrated traditional city in the country. Even if you are not interested in making any investment in Moroccan arts or crafts, a visit to Marrakesh is the experience of a lifetime. This great trade center at the base of the Atlas Mountains is the most famous traditional city in the country.

Many cruise lines have an all day tour, but it is very tiring. It takes about three to four hours each way by coach, and then you only have about five or six hours in the city. But it is time well spent. However, you do forego seeing any of Casablanca, so you must decide. If you are truly interested in the "real" traditional culture of Morocco, then Marrakesh is the city to visit. This is a major crossroads city where the more settled coastal and interior valley regions of Morocco come face to face with the sparsely settled regions of the Sahara. Marrakesh sits below the high Atlas Mountains and for centuries it had one foot in both worlds. To the present day, camel caravans still bring goods across the desert to the great marketplace in Marrakesh and then take back products that cannot easily be obtained in the deep interior. One vital product still transported is salt, a commodity needed by farm animals and people alike in rural areas where it is too costly to purchase commercial grade salt. And spices are still transported by camel caravan from eastern Africa through the Sahara to the great open market in Marrakesh.

Marrakesh is also where the two major cultural traditions of Morocco meet - Arab and Berber. Its old city is a kaleidoscope of colors, smells and sounds that are truly exotic. Unfortunately you will have such a limited time and your tour will be so structured that you will not be able to get off on your own to explore. And in this book, which is oriented toward the cruise ports, I do not go into any detail regarding what you will see in Marrakesh. I also do not make any recommendations for dining or shopping because you will not have any choices as to where you have lunch or are able to shop. The vast majority of you will not take this exciting, but very exhausting tour, if it is even offered by your cruise line. The best true way to visit Marrakesh is to do so as part of a land tour while visiting the country in general rather than on a one-day excursion from a cruise ship.

TANGIER: Far more western Mediterranean cruises will stop for a day in Tangier than those that will call in at Casablanca. When you look at the location of Tangier, it is along the primary route to places like Cadiz and Lisbon whereas Casablanca becomes a logical stop if the cruise itinerary includes the Canary Islands or is one taking in the west coast of Africa en route ultimately to Cape Town.

Tangier is located just outside the Strait of Gibraltar, facing northwest onto the open Atlantic Ocean. It is the second city of Morocco in population, having approximately 1,000,000 residents. And it has a fabled reputation for its colorful old quarter and as having been a city that saw many political intrigues during the 18th and 19th centuries, as European powers vied for control of North Africa.

Being a short ferry ride across the Straits of Gibraltar, many tourists who visit southern coastal ports in Spain will often include a day trip across by boat to visit Tangier. This gives them a taste of Islamic culture and enables them to say they have technically been to Africa.

GEOGRAPHIC SETTING: Tangier is a compact city that spreads outward and upward into the surrounding hills, as it wraps around a beautiful bay. The harbor is directly opposite the old walled section of the city known as the Medina. Beaches will be found both to the east and west of the harbor, which is of course man made. Tangier is known for its beautiful golden sand beaches that are similar to those of southern Spain and Portugal and lying within sight just across the Straits of Gibraltar. Only in Tangier the atmosphere is more exotic.

The climate is typically Mediterranean with cool, moist winters capable of supporting the same types of agriculture as found in Spain and Portugal. However, the growing of grapes is less pronounced since wine is not a traditional part of Islamic culture, actually prohibited by strict adherence to the faith. The hillsides are covered primarily in a scrub vegetation of low growing shrubs and gnarled trees, but one that is still quite beautiful. The Rif Mountains skirt just to the south of the city, and they are geologically related to the higher Atlas Mountains, which cannot be seen from Tangier.

BRIEF HISTORY: Tangier owes its founding to colonists from Carthage in the 5th century BCE. It later came under Roman domination in 146 BCE. In the 5th century AD, it was captured by the Vandals and then ultimately came under the authority of the Eastern Roman Empire, better known as Byzantium. By 702, it had become an Arab and Berber city.

In 1471, after one unsuccessful attempt, the Portuguese finally occupied Tangier and held it until 1662 when it was given to King Charles II of England. The gift was part of the wedding dowry when the king married the Portuguese king's daughter. In 1684, when attacked by the Moroccan sultan, the British evacuated, but not before blowing up their garrison and harbor installations.

When Morocco and the United States signed a diplomatic recognition treaty, the U. S. established its first consulate in Tangier while George Washington was still president. But during the early 19th century, both the British and French attempted to capture Tangier, but to no avail.

By the latter part of the 19th century, Tangier had become a meeting ground between Europe, the Middle East and Africa. Businessmen, spies, writers and expatriates called it home. It became a city of intrigues, murders, drug deals, smuggling and many other vices. And during World War II, it became a hotbed for spies from both sides. And as noted earlier, Morocco itself had come under the protection of Spain and France, with Spanish influence strongest in the north. In 1923, Tangier was internationalized and jointly administered by Britain, Spain and France. During the war, Spanish forces under orders from General Franco occupied Tangier, but they did not interfere with the British or French or other international activities. In 1956, the city was fully restored to the now independent Morocco and has remained so ever since. But it is still very international and heavily influenced by its role as a day-tripper's tourist activities. It is essentially the mainstay of the local economy.

WHAT TO SEE AND DO: Just as I did for Casablanca, I highly recommend either a ship sponsored coach tour or the use of a private car and driver/guide to explore Tangier. The city is highly congested, its streets are relatively narrow, especially in the Medina, and it is also very hilly, making walking a bit stressful for the vast majority of visitors. Yes you can negotiate with a taxi for a tour of the city, but remember this is a city that lives primarily off its daytime visitors coming by ferry or cruise ship. And not all taxi drivers will be forthright in giving you what you want or charging you a fair market price. Remember the old expression, "buyer be ware."

The major must see sights are not many, but it does take time to navigate the city. Here are the sights not to be missed:

* Medina - This is the old walled city adjacent to the port. It is fascinating, but very easy to become lost in because of its crooked narrow streets, steep hills and intense crowds. Having a guide definitely makes a difference between aimless wandering and enjoying the ultimate charm and flavor. If you are adventurous and do not mind the potential for getting lost then by all means explore the Medina on your own. I have done it and it is an experience to remember in a positive way.

* Kasbah - The name alone evokes visions of intrigue. This is a fortress and palace on the northern side of the Medina of Tangier. It is where the local sultan once lived and from where he ruled over the city. The Kasbah has a good museum and it also is high enough to offer good views over the Medina and the new city beyond. If you are on your own, I suggest starting at the Kasbah and then working your way downhill through the Medina.

* Souk - The traditional marketplace in any Islamic city is called the Souk. And inside the walled Medina of Tangier the souk is quite dominant. Yes it does sell a lot of souvenir items that tourists coming over for the day want. But if you look in its smaller lanes, you will find beautiful handmade brassware, Moroccan carpets and other ornaments of fine quality. And bargaining is a way of life, so never pay the asking price. Normally you should be able to cut that price in half.

* American Legation - The American Legation is considered a United States Historic Monument, the only one of its kind outside the country. It has a public museum that is open from 10 AM to 5 PM daily. And it is located at 8 Zankat America just south of the Medina and close to the Grand Mosque.

* Terrasse des Paresseux - Located atop a high hill in the old French Colonial part of the city, this viewpoint offers a striking view over the city of Tangier and across into Europe. You can enjoy a coffee or tea and take in the view, but once again be wary of all the hawkers selling souvenir items. It is a bit difficult to reach this plaza on foot, so it is normally a sight you see by private car or motor coach.

* Cape Spartel - About an hour drive outside of Tangier, this is the northwestern tip of Africa and has a stunning view over the Atlantic Ocean looking north to Portugal. There are also beautiful beaches below the cape. The only problem, as in so many tourist areas, is keeping the pesky vendors at bay so you can enjoy the vistas, the beach and the local architecture. I would not recommend venturing out by taxi. Only come if you have a private car or if your coach tour includes the stop.

DINING OUT: As in so many ports of call, the only meal you will be able to experience in Tangier is lunch. Most restaurants of quality are not open for lunch, and those that are can get quite busy. Being a city that caters to tourists who will in all likelihood never return, the best quality meals are not to be expected. For the most part, you are better off eating on board ship.

The best restaurant I can recommend for lunch is:
* Restaurant Rif Kebdani - Located in the Medina on Rue Dar Baroud and open from 11 AM onward, this is a good traditional restaurant that does pride itself in traditional Moroccan food. Chicken tagine with couscous is one of the best dishes to order.

SHOPPING: Hawkers selling "junk" will besiege you almost everywhere in Tangier unless you stroll off the main streets into quieter, traditional neighborhoods. This is true either in the Medina or in the newer parts of the city. For any serious shopping, as noted above, look for quality shops in the Souk within the walls of the Medina. Apart from the Souk, I have no specific shops to recommend for traditional handcrafts. If you have a guide with you it is in your favor, as they often have a good eye for quality and can then help you bargain.

FINAL NOTE: Tangier does in many ways live up to expectation. There is an exotic quality to the city and you can appreciate how it became a center for international business, smuggling and spying. But today it is more interested in catering to tourists, and in a way that does detract because of the constantly nagging feeling that you are being pressured into buying something.

The greater Casablanca area (© OpenStreetMap contributors)

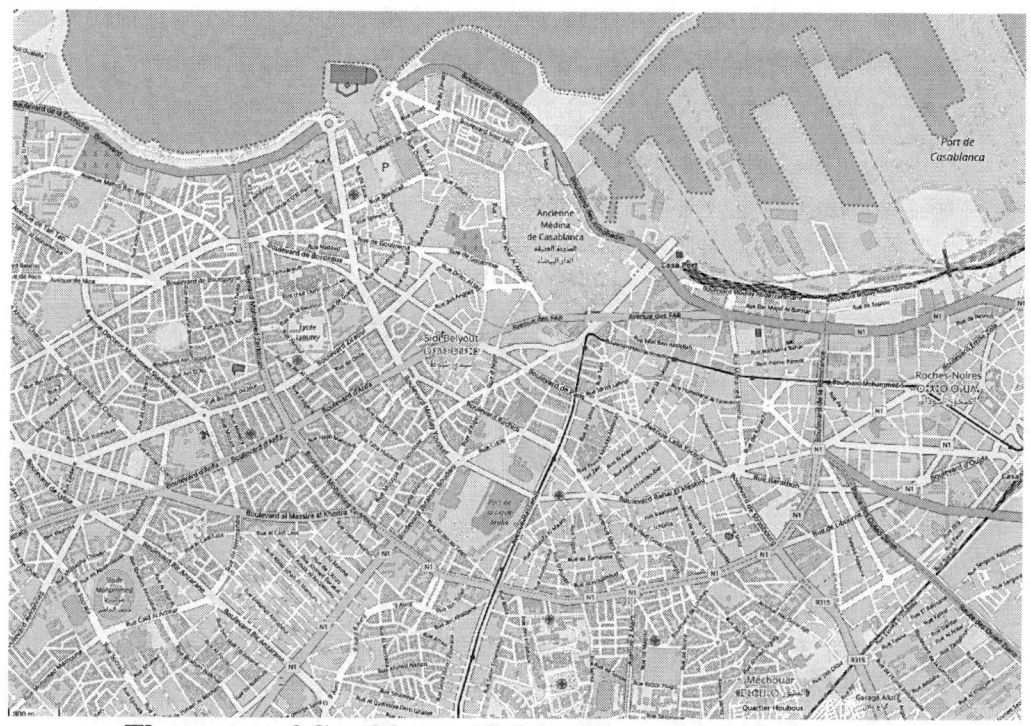

The center of Casablanca (© OpenStreetMap contributors)

The great Hassan II Mosque on the waterfront of Casablanca

A close up of the detailed carving on the Hassan II Mosqyue

Looking over the rooftops of Casablanca (Work of Иепей Максим Массалитиен, CC BY SA 2.0, Wikimedia.org)

Although touristy, most visitors to Casablanca want to see Rick's Cafe (Work of Didier55, CC BY SA 3.0, Wikimedia.org)

United Nations Square in the heart of modern Casaablanca

Mohammed V Square in the heart of Casablanca

Boulevard du Paris in central Casablanca

Boulevard d'Anfa in the upmarket southwest end of Casablanca

A typical northeast Casablanca neighborhood

A street bazaar in one of the northeastern poor suburbs of Casablanca

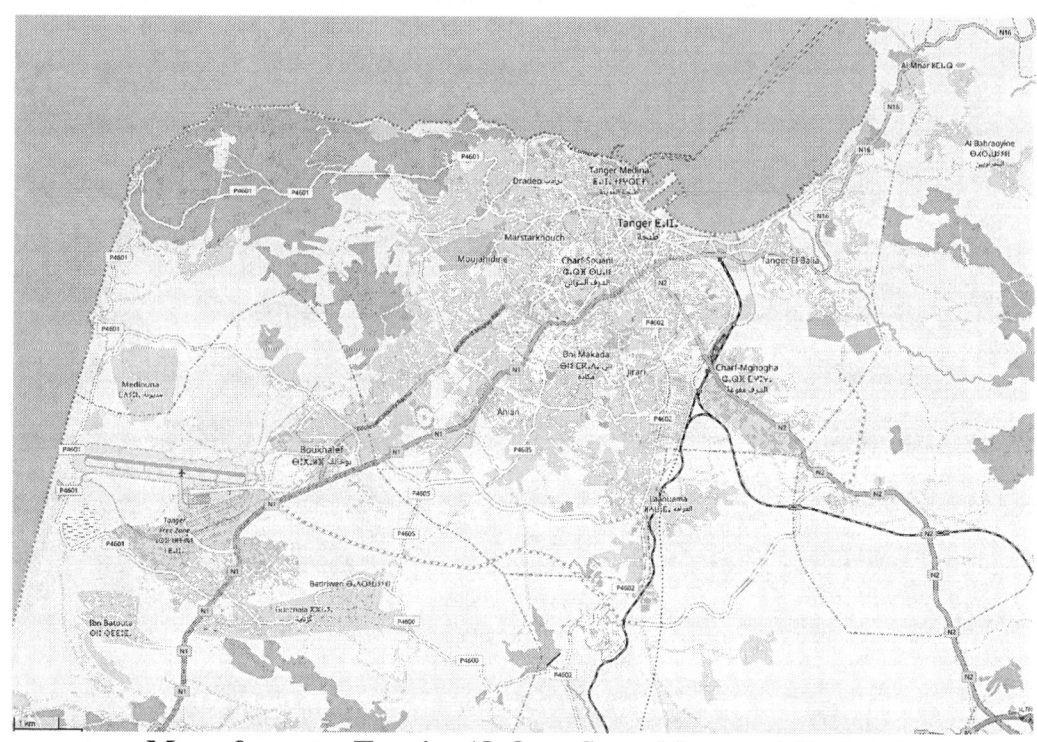

Map of greaterTangier (© OpenStreetMap contributors)

Map of central Tangier (© OpenStreetMap contributors)

A view of the Medina of Tangier from offshore (Work of Hedwig Storch, CC BY SA 3.0, Wikimedia.org)

The contrasts of Tangier (Work of cat_collector, CC BY SA 2.0, Wikimedia.org)

The beachfront of modern Tangier (Work of Calflier001, CC BY SA 2.0, Wikimedia.org)

Entrance to the Kasbah in the Tangier Medina

A typical street in the Tangier Medina

The Tangier Medina has the flavor of centuries past

MAJOR PORT OF CALL IN PORTUGAL

A map of Portugal

Portugal is a Mediterranean country both in terms of its physical geography and its culture and history. But Portugal is actually located outside of the Straits of Gibraltar and is technically an Atlantic country, facing south and west onto the open ocean. But so many western Mediterranean cruises will either begin or terminate in Lisbon, and therefore it must be considered as part of the western Mediterranean in the broad sense. There are a few more specialized cruises on the smaller upmarket cruise lines such as Seabourn or Silversea that will on occasion also stop in Portomaõ on the southern Algarve coast of Portugal. Some cruise itineraries that begin in the Mediterranean travel well beyond the Straits of Gibraltar to such destinations as Madeira, the Azores or Canary Islands, but these are far more than Mediterranean cruises. For the purposes of this book, only Lisbon and Portomaõ are being considered.

THE NATURE OF PORTUGAL: The country of Portugal shares only a border with Spain on the north and east and then faces the Atlantic Ocean on the south and west. Portugal only occupies 92,212 square kilometers or 35,603 square miles and has a population of 10,450,000. It has actually lost a small portion of its population to out migration in recent years. The land area and population also include the Azores and Madeira Island located well out to sea from the mainland. Its border of 1,214 kilometers or 754 miles with Spain is the longest land border of any two nations within the European Union.

Like most of the Mediterranean region, Portugal is a semi-arid country experiencing cool, wet winters and hot, dry summers. The vegetation is primarily arranged in a scrub woodland pattern with some stands of pine in the highest elevations. The country is quite rugged, with moderately high hills and mountains in the west, and its highest elevations along the Spanish border to the east. Two major rivers, the Duoro in the north and the Tagus in the center, both flowing west to the Atlantic. With a moderate climate, Portugal is capable of raising a variety of grains, vegetables and fruit and nut orchards. Olives are an important crop for both the fruit and for high quality oil. Portugal also has a significant acreage of grapes to produce fine quality wines.

Portugal is an ancient country, having been populated well before the advancement of the Romans. The Visigoths and Moors at one time occupied much of its land to ultimately be expelled during the Reconquista. Later it became a major power along with Spain in the late 15th and early 16th centuries, being one of the two major explorers and colonizers in the Americas. It was Portugal that settled Brazil, Angola and Mozambique as well as having established an early foothold in India and Southeast Asia.

In 1755, a massive earthquake ravaged Lisbon, destroying much of its infrastructure, a catastrophe from which it never fully recovered. In the early 19th century, Napoleonic forces invaded the country, forcing King John to flee to Brazil and establishing a government in exile for the entire empire. When Napoleon was defeated, King John returned to Lisbon, leaving his son Dom

Pedro in charge of Brazil only to find that in 1822, his son declared himself the king of Brazil, independent from Portugal.

A weakened Portugal was never able to reclaim its power and prestige or its great sources of wealth. In 1910, a revolution ended the monarchy only to fall into dictatorship that lasted until 1974. By this time, both Angola and Mozambique had declared their independence, and ultimately Portugal relinquished its claims to Goa in western India, Macao near Hong Kong and Timor in the Indonesian Archipelago. Despite these losses to the nation, its legacy remains and with the immense size and population of Brazil, the Portuguese language and culture are quite alive and well in the Western Hemisphere. And in southern Africa, a mixed legacy of Portuguese occupation remains.

Modern Portugal is small, highly dependent upon agricultural exports and tourism as major elements of its economy. It is a member of the European Union, but one of the weaker partners economically. But overall the people do live quite well and they have a spirit that makes it an attractive place for many English-speaking expatriates to settle in retirement.

In 2001, the country took the boldest step of any nation in Europe. Portugal legalized the individual possession of all formerly illicit drugs, and the result was only a small increase is use, but a very drastic decrease in violent crimes. But to date no other country has been as willing to take such a step.

LISBON:
Portugal's great city and center of both culture and government is Lisbon, built on a series of hills north of the broad estuary of the River Tagus. This is a city of great visual color, as when it was rebuilt after the 1755 earthquake, people continued with the tradition of whitewashed plaster buildings with red ceramic tile roofs. On a bright morning, the city seems to glitter in the sunlight, as the older neighborhoods climb the hills on both sides of the small lowland plain where the city center is located. With a population of 2,800,000, more than 20 percent of the people of Portugal live in its metropolitan area.

The inner city of Lisbon is one of the more traditional of European cities. There are no high-rise buildings or modern constructs. After the great 1755 earthquake, the waterfront was rebuilt with a major plaza facing the River Tagus, bilaterally encased in magnificent public buildings. From this massive square a grid pattern of streets extends north through the flatland known as Baixa that separates the hillside neighborhoods of Alfama and Mourana to the east and Chiado and Barrio Alto to the west. The grand medieval Castelo de

Sao Jorge commands the highest hill in Alfama. The grand tree lined divided boulevard of Avenida de Liberdade leads north to a great roundabout behind which is the Park Eduardo VII with its commanding view back down the boulevard to the heart of the old city. To the west, occupying several thousand acres of hilly terrain is the massive Parque Floristal de Montsanto, a park that is in good measure composed of the wild, natural vegetation.

There are very few flat areas to Lisbon, the streets therefore conforming more to the local topography, lending distinct individualism to the various districts that each seems to be somewhat independent of the other. And interconnecting many of the major streets is a network of trams (streetcars) that are quite tiny, operating on narrow track and capable of negotiating the steep streets and drastic curves. At times you think these little cars will scrape the sides of the buildings, but they somehow do not. Underneath central Lisbon, however, there is a quite modern Metro that aids greatly in relieving inner city congestion.

A BRIEF LISBON HISTORY: The site of the city was inhabited by Stone Age tribes for thousands of years prior to the start of western historical records. Around 1200 BCE there is evidence that Phoenicians did maintain a trading post near what is now Baixa. After the Romans defeated the Carthaginians in 146 BCE, they began systematic settlement of the Iberian Peninsula to deny Carthage access to what had been its most important territory. What is now Lisbon was an important Roman regional center, but after the fall of Rome, it was the so-called barbarian tribes from what are now Germany and the center of Europe.

In the year 711, Islamic forces captured Lisbon and occupied it until 1147 when the Portuguese King Alfonso liberated the city. During the Muslim or Moorish period, Jews and Christians were both integrated into the community, but after the Reconquista, members of the Islamic faith and Jews were forced to convert, flee or die. By the 1500's, Portugal had become a major world power with colonies from Southeast Asia to Africa to Brazil. And Lisbon as capital of this vast empire became a rich and grand city. The Portuguese added many far flung elements to their architecture, and Lisbon's cathedrals, monasteries and palaces took on a very distinctive aura. To this day, there are many very distinct differences between Portuguese and Spanish architecture, with the Portuguese being far more colorful. The summer capital of the royal family was Sintra, a mountaintop small city west of Lisbon that is still a popular destination to the present.

In 1580, the Portuguese and Spanish kingdoms were merged and it was not until 1640 that Portugal was again able to break away from Spanish Hapsburg rule. The ultimate disaster that began the process of bringing down Lisbon as a powerful city was the earthquake of 1755, followed in the early 1900's by the Napoleonic invasion and then by King John VI's son splitting Brazil from Portugal in 1821.

In the late 19th and early 20th centuries, Lisbon saw many new parks; public buildings and institutions of higher learning develop. During World War II, the city became a meeting place for spies from both sides as well as a haven for over 100,000 refuges fleeing Nazi oppression. Following the war, with a dictatorial government under General António Salazar, Portugal ultimately lost its African colonies to the independence movement, and finally in 1974, a revolution toppled the dictator. Today Lisbon is one of the most beloved cities in the European Union for holidays, conventions, diplomatic meetings and cultural events. It was designated the European Capital of Culture in 1994 and is visited today by several million tourists per year.

WHAT TO SEE AND DO: Most cruise passengers visiting Lisbon will either be arriving to join a ship or disembarking after a western Mediterranean or Madeira, Azores or Canary Island cruise. Only a few cruise ships pass through Lisbon en route between England and the western Mediterranean, as part of a longer cruise, often when ships are being repositioned. If your visit is part of an embarkation or debarkation, you should plan on spending at least two to three days in the city, as there is much to see and enjoy. Either flying in and going directly to your ship or heading home upon debarkation is doing a great disservice to yourself by not taking time to enjoy Lisbon.
Only cruise itineraries where Lisbon is simply a port call will offer tours through the city or into the surrounding countryside, especially to Sintra or the beach resorts of Estoril or Cascais. For those of you who will be staying in a hotel, you can arrange to join a group tour or have the concierge obtain a car and driver/guide for at least one day to enable you to explore beyond your ability to walk through the city center.

Here are my recommendations as to the must see sights of Lisbon:
* The Alfama - This ancient hillside district just east of the main city square dates back to the time of the Visigoths, Moors and early years of the Portuguese kingdom. Its winding and often narrow streets are lined with many colorful houses, most with red tile roofs. Fortunately many buildings did survive the 1755 earthquake, making this the most sought after part of the city for its natural charm. Most group tours will include the Alfama with many of the viewpoints overlooking the city center, but you can also visit this area on your own either by private car, taxi or using one of the narrow yellow trams. This should be everybody's first stop when starting to tour the city.

* **Castelo de São Jorge** - Atop the highest hill in the Alfama sits this rather forbidding walled fortress that dates back to the Moorish conquest of Portugal. It was the military and royal fortress that ruled over the surrounding countryside. Today it is the most historic site in the city, and it offers the best of all viewpoints over the city.
* **Praca do Comercio** - The center of Lisbon since the reconstruction after the 1755 earthquake, the Praca is a magnificent and monumental public square surrounded by what was intended to be the commercial heart of the city. And it does house many beautiful shops, still the focal hub of Lisbon.
* **Chiado** - North of the Praca do Comercio is Chiado, the city's other great square and a wonderful place to enjoy the architecture as it enfolds you when you stand in this grand square. This is also the most fashionable shopping area of the city and the place to see and be seen.
* **Barrio Alto** - Located west of the city center, Barrio Alto is on the opposite side of the Alfama. Most of the area was rebuilt after the great 1755 earthquake, and today it is the true downtown of Lisbon with regard to having its narrow streets that climb steep hillsides crammed with shops, cafes and nightclubs. This is the most vibrant and exciting part of the city and one can explore for days if they had the time. But for ship passengers, it is a must if only for an hour.
* **Ajuda National Palace** - This is the former royal palace of the Portuguese monarchy. Surprisingly it is rarely crowded, yet it offers an opportunity to view its richly decorated rooms, artistic treasures and garner a feel for the one time majesty of this former royal residence. It is located in suburban Belem and easy to reach by car or taxi from Barrio Alto.
* **Mosteiro dos Jeronimos** - This is a massive and magnificent example of gothic architecture, dating to 1502, it was once a major monastery, but today is still venerated and visited by Portuguese pilgrims. It is also the burial site for Vasco da Gama, Portugal's great navigator and explorer. The monastery is not to be missed, and it is located facing the Praca do Imperio on the River Tagus just west of the heart of the city.
* **Torre de Belem** - Just west of the great monastery and along the River Tagus is the Torre de Belem. This is a rather ornate 16th century monument to the great age of discovery when Portugal was almost the master of the sea, as its explorers ventured around Africa to Southeast Asia and across the Atlantic to found Brazil.t
* **Parque Eduardo VII** - Located north of the city center, this grand park is reached via the beautiful divided boulevard known as Avenida do Liberdade. At the upper end of the park, you gain a dramatic perspective looking across the greenery, down the avenida all the way to the waterfront.

Apart from the major sites listed above within the city, I highly recommend that you spend the second half of the day visiting Sintra. This is the old royal summer capital city, located atop a collection of hills that reach a maximum of 175 meters or 574 feet above sea level. The hills are thickly wooded, giving the various small districts of Sintra a leafy aura, just what you would expect for a summer respite. In 1174, after Lisbon fell from Moorish control under the Reconquista, it once again began to flourish as the summer residence for Portuguese nobility and royalty. It saw its largest expansion during the 18th and 19th centuries with the construction of romantic style palaces and villas. Today it is a UNESCO World Heritage Site, and worthy of a visit. It takes about one hour to drive to the heart of Sintra from Lisbon.

On the return, take the coast road through Cascais and Estoril, two magnificent seaside communities that also date back to the 12th century. Today both are home to the wealthy class of Lisbon, and are considered to be prime residential suburbs each with many buildings of historic charm and interest. A drive to Sintra, returning through Cascais and Estoril will take three to four hours, and should only be undertaken if you feel content with what you first saw in Lisbon.

Essentially it takes more than one full day in Lisbon to really begin to understand the history, charm and true beauty of this city and it environs. But if your cruise begins or ends in Lisbon, you should plan on a few days to take in the sights.

DINING OUT: Portuguese cuisine is an experience that will add to the overall pleasure of a day spent in Lisbon. Many of you will be arriving in Lisbon to board your ship, others will be debarking, and I trust in both cases you will allow a few days to explore the city. But many cruise itineraries only make a port call. I am only recommending a few superior restaurants open for lunch, based upon the port call. For those staying over in Lisbon, your hotel concierge can recommend and help you book fine dining establishments for dinner. I am starting with a Lisbon institution that is very popular in the morning hours.
* Pasteis de Cerveja de Belem - Small tarts filled with a custard cream and dusted with powdered sugar and served with coffee or tea are a traditional morning treat in Lisbon. But there is supposedly only one place that makes the original tarts, and this is it. Located along the River Tagus at Rua de Belem # 15, and open from 7 AM to 8 PM, this is a morning must. Pass through the noisy and crowded take away bakery and into one of many dining rooms where you can then order a tray of these delectable treats. Most people can eat four to six at one sitting; so don't worry about the calories or cholesterol, as you will walk that off during the day. Indulge this one time!
* Frade dos Mares - Located at Avenida Dom Carlos I #55 and open from Noon to 3 PM, this is an outstanding restaurant for lunch where you will be

able to sample traditional Portuguese cuisine. One of my favorites is cod, a staple in Portuguese cooking for centuries. Before refrigeration, bacalao, the salted cod was a basic staple, but today it is a delicacy. But fresh cod is generally the rule along with sea bass and many types of shellfish. Have the ship concierge or your driver make a table booking.

* Augusto Lisboa - Located on Rua de Santa Marinha #26 and open from 10 AM onward until evening, this is a delightful restaurant serving lighter fare, but still very traditional, like eating in someone's home. Great soups, sandwiches, light entrees and sinful desserts.

* Maruto Bar and Bistro - Found on Rua do Cais de Santarem #30 and open from 11 AM onward, this is a great place to enjoy a refreshing beer or wine cooler and sample Portuguese tapas. You choose from a great variety of these small snack like appetizers and keep eating until you are full. Tapas are a traditional lunch item in both Portugal and Spain, and you will find them quite satisfying.

* Frangasquiera Nacional - Located on Rua da Imprensa Nacional #116 and open from 12:30 to 2:30 PM for lunch, this is another outstanding restaurant where you can taste traditional Portuguese cuisine. This is a small restaurant that also offers take away food service, and it is primarily a traditional asado or grill similar to what is so famous in Brazil. It gives you a chance to sample a hearty meatier type of Portuguese fare.

* da Prata 52 - Located on Rua de Prata #52, as the name indicates, this is an outstanding restaurant for very elegant Portuguese luncheon, and its selection of seafood dishes is excellent. A reservation would be suggested in advance.

SHOPPING: For those who want to shop, I recommend that you confine your explorations to only those artistic and craft items that represent Portuguese culture. In the city center's fine shops you will only see the same types of quality merchandise you will be seeing or have seen in other Mediterranean resort destinations. There is just too much to see in Lisbon to spend time shopping for anything but Portuguese objects d'art or fine craft. I have no personal favorites to recommend because I frankly have not seen anything special that I wanted to buy in the way of traditional crafts. I suggest you ask your guide if you have a private car and have a desire to spend time shopping.

FINAL NOTE: As your ship sails down the River Tagus your only regret will be that you did not have more time in Lisbon. However, if your cruise began or ended in Lisbon, then you should plan to linger for a couple of days at the very least.

PORTIMÃO:
Located on the southern coast of Portugal in the former kingdom and present day region of the Algarve, Portimão is the

principal destination for those cruise itineraries that include this part of the country. The current population of approximately 56,000 belies the importance of this city as a major tourist destination. When looking at the beachfront, all one sees are high-rise apartments and hotels, far more than the local inhabitants would require. Thus tourism is a major and vital part of the economy, and because of its beautiful beaches and tourist infrastructure, many cruise lines do offer a one-day port call in Portimão.
The Algarve has a long and rich history that has added to the overall architectural and cultural flavor of this most southern part of Portugal, which also has the country's most equitable and genuine Mediterranean climate.

In 711, the Moors took control of southern Portugal along with southern Spain, developing the region into a powerful, yet enlightened kingdom. By the 13th century, the Kingdom of Portugal had won back the Algarve in a series of bloody battles. Ultimately by the 15th century, the Portuguese were controlling segments of North Africa as part of their broader Kingdom of Portugal and the Algarve. In 1755, the great earthquake that destroyed much of Lisbon also heavily damaged many of the towns along the coast of the Algarve, but primarily resulting from a tsunami spawned by the earthquake. It was not until the Portuguese Republic was proclaimed in 1910, that the term Algarve was dropped from the name.

Today the Algarve is the most important source of tourist revenue to all of Portugal, and it is also home to thousands of expatriates primarily from the United Kingdom.

Portimão is not the largest or most important city of the Algarve, but it is one of its most beautiful and popular and for that reason many cruise lines have included it in their itinerary. The Visigoths inhabited Portimão as far back as the 5th century, and then the Moors conquered it in the early 8th century. Ultimately it came under Portuguese rule in the 13th century. But it was never a major center for administration, but it was important for its exports of figs, olives, olive oil and fish products. It was also an important center for the importation of slaves from Africa and sugar from Brazil. But the 1755 earthquake nearly destroyed the city and it lost much of its significance after this catastrophic event.

Modern Portimão owes its existence to foreigners discovering its beautiful beaches in the early 20th century, the first wave so to speak. Prior to the tourist influx, a fish processing plant kept the city economically on the edge of viability, but it collapsed and had it not been for tourism, Portimão may never have recovered.

WHAT TO SEE AND DO: Almost all activities in Portimão are related to the beach and the sea. There are few sites of great historic significance because of the destruction wrought by the 1755 earthquake and tsunami. Rather than trying to tire yourself out exploring the city or the countryside, I strongly urge you to just relax and take in the beaches, have a good meal and save your energy either for Lisbon if heading north or for the Spanish ports if heading into the Mediterranean. The beaches of Portimão are not right in the heart of the city, as Portimão has developed as a port on the Arade River estuary. The beaches are a short distance to the south, the largest and most important one being that of Praia Alvor. Most cruise lines will generally operate a shuttle bus to the beach, as there is little of interest for visitors in the center of Portimão.

Here is my list of sights not to be missed in Portimão:
* Praia da Rocha - The main beach on the southern margin of Portimão, here the golden sand makes for a pleasant atmosphere in which to enjoy the sun or water sports. There are also many cafes and shops lining the beach, providing for all tourist needs. The beach itself still also has a bit of a wild appearance, and there are rock outcrops, caves and sea stacks to lend beauty to the surroundings.
* Alvor Boardwalk - This is an approximately two-kilometer boardwalk that runs along the beach. It is only now developing, thus there are a few cafes and other services. But it is primarily a walkway for people who live in the various apartment or gated community complexes to come out and stroll, taking in the cool sea air. Sometimes it is jokingly called the "senior citizen boardwalk" for good measure.
* Museo de Portimão - Located in the city on Rua D. Carlos, this small museum tells the history of the region through its many displays. It is open from 10 AM to 6 PM daily and worthy of your time if you are interested in how this region came to be the tourist haven it is today.
* Monumentos Megaliticas de Alcalar - This site is located north of Alvor and would require a private car and driver or taxi unless it is included by your cruise line on a tour. It is essentially a living museum of the Paleolithic or Old Stone Age and Neolithic or New Stone Age settlement long before the Visigoths settled the region. It is a good site to visit after visiting the museum noted above, but only if ancient archaeology is of interest to you.
* Town of Alvor - Adjacent to Portimão on its western margin is the town of Alvor, which dates back even earlier than Portimão, having first been established by ancient Carthage in 436 AD. There are fine examples of 17th century to present day Portuguese architecture, plus the partial remains of the old medieval castle. If you are doing the Alvor Boardwalk, you can continue on into the town of Alvor either by private car and driver or taxi. It is a very pleasant community.

DINING OUT: Since cruise ship port calls are generally eight hours or less, the only meal that can be recommended is lunch. And as I did with Lisbon, I am only recommending a choice few restaurants that serve traditional Portuguese cuisine. Here are my choices:

* **Solar de Farelo** - Located at Varzea do Farelo in Portimão, and open from Noon to 4 PM for lunch, this is a traditional restaurant whose menu represents the many dishes typical of the Algarve. It has an outstanding reputation for its freshness and quality.

* **Restaurante Atlantida** - Located in Alvor along Praia Tres Irmaos, this is an outstanding seafood restaurant with a breathtaking view of the sea and cliffs.

* **O Luis** - Located in Alvor along Praia Dos Tres Imãos and open from 9 AM onward, this is another excellent seafood restaurant situated right on the beach. It has a diverse menu and also a nice bar for those who want to start with libations before lunch.

* **A Ribiera** - In Alvor at Rua da Ribeira #15, this restaurant specializes in fresh seafood prepared in the traditional manner of the Algarve. It opens at 11 AM and remains open all day. The atmosphere is more of a country inn, but unfortunately it does have TV in its bar area, detracting from the ambiance. But the food quality is what counts.

SHOPPING: I have no recommendations because the Portimão shops are for the most part catering to tourists and winter residents. The orientation is more toward upmarket jewelry and clothing. I have never seen any craft items that I would consider genuine and representative of the traditions of the Algarve.

FINAL NOTES: Visiting the Algarve can be considered a treat, as this has become such an in demand tourist hot spot in Portugal. However, you will find that it is becoming so developed that it is slowly loosing its Portuguese flavor since during the winter months tourists and expatriates outnumber locals.

Map of greater Lisbon (© OpenStreetMap contributors)

Map of the metro area of Lisbon (© OpenStreetMap contributors)

Map of the city center of Lisbon (© OpenStreetMap contributors)

Flying over Lisbon, looking south (Work of Guillaume Baviere, CC BY SA 2.0, Wikimedia.org

A view to the city center from the Alfam

A view to the west from an Alfama vantage point

A view to the northwest from an Alfama vantage point

A view of the main hillside of the Alfama

In the heart of the Alfama

The heart of the Praca Comercio in Baixia

Rua Augusta in the heart of Praca Comercio

Along Rossio Square in the city center

The Praca Rossio in the city center

Daily life on Chiado Plaza

The National Parliament of Portugal

The great Monasterio dos Jeronimos in Belem

Inside the famous Belem Bakery

The old summer royal capital of Sintra

One of the many hillside smaller palaces in Sintra

The National Palace in Sintra

In the town center of Cascais

Coming into the town of Estoril

A map of greater Portimão (© OpenStreetMap contributors)

The beachfront in Portimão (Work of Steven Fruitsmaak, CC BT SA 3.0, Wikimedia.org)

The modern side of Portimão (Work of Jose A, CC BY SA 2.0, Wikimedia.org)

The traditional side of Portimão (Work of Notifly, CC BY SA 4.0, Wikimedia.org)

MAJOR PORTS OF CALL IN SPAIN

A map of Spain

Spain is one sought after country in the western portion of the Mediterranean Sea. There are more potential ports of call for the various cruise itineraries offered in this part of Europe. Spain is a large country geographically, extending over 509,990 square kilometers or 195,364 square miles. And the population today is approximately 46,500,000. Spain is both a Mediterranean and Atlantic nation with seacoasts on both bodies of water. But the core of the country is in the interior, centering upon its capital and largest city of Madrid.

SPANISH LANDSCAPES: Spain is a very spectacular country with a rim of mountains bordering both of its coasts, and a large central plateau that is crossed by additional ranges of mountains. The highest peaks of mainland Spain are located in the Sierra Nevada, a snowcapped range along its southern Mediterranean coast. Its highest peak is 3,478 meters or 11,410 feet. But the highest mountain in what is Spain the nation lies on the island of Tenerife in the Canary Islands off the west coast of Africa. El Teide Volcano is 3,718 meters or 12,198 feet high. The Pyrenees Mountains form a rather significant barrier wall between Spain and France, and their highest peak straddles the border of the two nations, standing 3,404 meters or 11,168 feet high.

Apart from being blessed with high mountains that catch and hold winter snow, releasing the water to provide for numerous rivers that flow outward toward either the Atlantic or Mediterranean. These mountains have also provided the Spanish people with thick coniferous forests, and even today there are still major stands of pine and hardwoods. But they are properly managed and Spain provides national parks for its citizens to enjoy.

The climate of the country can be divided into three specific categories:
* The Mediterranean Coastal Climate is typically mild and moist during the winter months, but hot and dry in summer. Agriculture is capable in those areas where the land is sufficiently level enough for crops or orchards. Spain is a major producer of wine, citrus, olives, a variety of vegetable and other orchard crops. And people from northern latitudes see the Mediterranean coast as being blessed with sunshine, warmth and beautiful beaches. Thus the coast is the center of one of the largest tourist industries in the entire Mediterranean basin.
* The semi-arid interior plateaus represent the heartland of Spain. Here there is more limited rainfall or snow, yet sufficient to have spawned a great empire. The summers are hot but punctuated by thundershowers, as moist air is drawn up over the high mountains. Winters can be cold and blustery, but tolerable.
* The Atlantic Coast where the climate is more maritime similar to France and the southern part of Great Britain. Summers are cool, damp and often foggy while winters can be cold, blustery and rainy. This is a part of Spain that most foreign visitors are essentially unaware of.

A SHORT SPANISH HISTORY: Spain was once the most powerful nation in Europe. From the 15th through the early 19th centuries, its empire extended from the western mountains of the North American continent all the way to the southern tip of South America. In addition, Spain had colonies in the Caribbean and far western Pacific Ocean basin and briefly held territories in northern Africa. One often wonders how a country not overly blessed with natural resources became so powerful. Any of you who live in the southwestern regions of the United States from California east to Texas are living on what was once Spanish soil, and later became the Mexican Republic. The strong Hispanic influence in this part of the country is the result of initial Spanish colonization, thus it is safe to say that Spain has had a profound impact on a large segment of American culture. And all of Latin America owes its existence to Spanish colonization.

The Greek and Carthaginian establishment of small trading settlements along the coast marks the start of Iberian history. By 250 BCE, the Romans began their drive to conquer the land, and it was the Roman cultural influence that brought a modicum of unity to the diverse Celtic, Basque and Iberian cultures such as the fusion of Latin into the native tongues. Spanish and Portuguese are after all Romanic languages.

Spain was one of the earlier countries of Europe into which Christianity was introduced. Today the Spanish and Portuguese languages along with a very traditional Catholic church are so much a part of the Iberian identity.

As Rome began to collapse, various Germanic tribes pushed their conquests deep into the peninsula. The most dominant were the Vandals. At the same time as the Germanic tribes were moving south, the Byzantines began to establish settlements along the coast where first Greek and Carthaginians once had settled. The most important event began in 711 when the Islamic Moors swept cross from northern Africa and by 718 occupied most of the peninsula.

The Moors changed Spain in so many ways that are still seen and heard today. Spanish and Portuguese music, art, architecture and cuisine all bear the mark of the Moors. And it was then taken to the Americas where it became rooted as well. The Moors were very tolerant of both Christian and Jewish communities that had previously developed across Iberia, contributing to the overall cultural mix. The heart of the Moorish empire was in the valleys of southern Spain, what became known as Andalusia. Three cities stood out as the centers of Islamic culture and architectural achievement - Córdoba, Seville and Granada. These cities were so magnificent that after the fall of the Moorish empire in Iberia, no other European cities would match their sophistication and beauty again.

The Reconquista was the historic period of ongoing warfare between Christian forces and the Moors that began in 722 and finally ended in 1492 when the combined armies of the new Christian kingdoms of Castile and Aragon were able to crush the Islamic Kingdom of Granada. But the other major cities of Córdoba and Seville had fallen to the Christian armies earlier. The Christian forces had taken the heartland of Spain around Madrid during the 12th century, and the new kingdoms grew in power and wealth. But during the 13th century, the Black Plague had brought near havoc to most of Christian Spain. Today we can understand the reasons why the Islam communities suffered far less by looking at the differences in lifestyles. The Islamic communities were far cleaner and had running water whereas the Christian cities and towns were essentially breeding grounds for disease due to their crowded and filthy living conditions.

When the Moors were finally driven from Spain, the communities of Jews who had flourished were given the ultimatum to convert to Catholicism or perish. Most chose to flee, and they followed their Moorish cousins into North Africa and the Middle East, becoming what are called the Sephardic Jews in social contrast to the Jews of Europe.

It was the combined Kingdoms of Aragon and Castile that unified Spain with their two famous monarchs, Ferdinand II of Aragon and Isabella of Castile. And they provided the financial backing for the expeditions of Christopher Columbus to the New World, marking what would become the largest colonial empire of all times. The fabulous wealth that would be later brought back to Spain by such conquerors as Hernán Cortés who destroyed the Aztec of México and Francisco Pizarro who conquered the great Inca Empire would make this the most celebrated country of Europe, and also the most feared. Spanish monarchs held great sway in Rome and it is said that the Pope was essentially a Spanish puppet. This can be seen at its most famous best when Henry XII of England wanted to divorce his first wife Katherine of Aragon because she could not bear a son. The Spanish king put so much pressure on the Pope as to have him reject the annulment, causing Henry to create the Church of England.

But King Henry's divorce ultimately led to the downfall of the naval might of Spain when King Philip II wanted to lay siege to England. His armada of ships was destroyed by a combination of stormy weather in the English Channel and the tenacity of the British navy to defend its shores. After this period, Spain was no longer the unchallenged master of Europe.

In the early 18th century, the War of the Spanish Succession brought about the start of Spain's ultimate decline. In 1700, Charles II of Spain, the last Habsburg king, died without leaving an heir. Charles had chosen Duke Philip of Anjou who was King Louis VIV of France's second oldest grandson. This would be putting a member of the House of Bourbon on the throne, an act that many other crowned heads found unsatisfactory, as it would give Louis XIV too great a command over Europe. King Louis was pleased to have his grandson named, as it put Spain and France only one heir apart from being joined as one vast nation. England, the Dutch Republic and Austria along with the states of the Holy Roman Empire supported it Emperor Leopold I, a Habsburg, as their choice. The Treaty of Utrecht in 1714 brought the war to a close. Spain lost control of its European territory bordering the Dutch

Republic and it had to renounce any future claim to the French throne, but it did keep its American colonial empire.

The final blow to Spanish greatness came in the early 19th century when one by one its colonies in the Americas began to revolt against the iron hand of control from Madrid. It all began in 1821 when México declared and fought for its independence. And then by the 1850's all of Latin America except Cuba and Puerto Rico had become independent. And in 1898 when Spain and the United States became embroiled in conflict, Spain ended up loosing its two Caribbean colonies plus the Philippines in southeastern Asia.

During the Napoleonic Wars, Spain made several blunders, which enabled Napoleon to indirectly rule briefly through his brother Joseph Bonaparte. The Spanish people were outraged, and in 1808 they rebelled against Napoleonic control. Fortunately the British did intervene, as Napoleon's forces were for the most part engaged in Russia. In 1814, the Bourbon King Ferdinand VII was returned to the throne. But King Ferdinand made a drastic mistake that would ultimately cause Spain to engage in an all out civil war. During the Napoleonic Wars, a Spanish council called the Cortes of Cádiz was formed to represent all of the Empire. In 1812, its intent was to represent the Spanish Empire along with the king in a constitutional form of government with the king as head of state, just as was seen in Britain. But King Ferdinand refused and held on to absolute power, a form of monarchy that would ultimately bring down the Habsburgs of Austria-Hungary and the Romanoff Dynasty of Russia.

Ultimately in 1868, there was a revolution in Spain that established a Spanish Republic, which was very unstable and went through so five presidents acting as head of state and two prime ministers in just six years. Finally in 1874, the Bourbon crown was restored, but with a congress serving alongside. No longer was Spain an absolute monarchy.

With the loss of all of its colonial holdings in the Americas and with the Philippines and Guam taken away in the Pacific, Spain turned inward, developing its economy and restoring itself to a modicum of prosperity. But empire still had its fascination and did join other European powers in the taking of territory in Africa. By the time of World War I in Europe, Spain had managed to lay claim to Western Sahara and Equatorial Guinea and also became the dominant power over Morocco.

In 1931, the Second Spanish Republic was created and the House of Bourbon was again removed in favor of a Republic. This short-lived republic did give localized autonomy to such regions as the Basque territory, Catalonia and Galicia, areas where the cultures were very traditional and not in effect Spanish. Even today there is a strong degree of cultural distinctness to these three northern regions and there are still strong wishes among large numbers for political autonomy. Although very well supported by the population at large, there was a strong left wing movement in Spain that favored tighter control over the government and military in what could be today labeled as Fascist. And ultimately the differences between left and right plunged Spain into a brutal civil war that lasted from 1936 to 1939, concurrent with the rise of Hitler in Germany and Mussolini in Italy. Generalisimo Francisco Franco and his left wing forces were the victors, having received help from Germany, Italy and Portugal. The Republican forces had nominal support from the Soviet Union and aid from thousands of multinationals that came as volunteers. Had the rest of Europe not been poised for war with the threats and advances made by the Nazi, the powers such as France, Britain and possibly the United States may have come to the aid of the Republicans. This was an all out war with devastation wrought to many cities and towns and a loss of life that is estimated at over 500,000 plus that many more leaving the country. Some say it was a prelude to World War II.

When war came to the rest of Europe, Generalismio Franco remained neutral, not because he felt a lack of loyalty to Nazi Germany, but because his country was too weak to participate in a global conflict. Franco turned his attention to reforming the country, which from his perspective meant demands for reforms of the Catholic Church, repression of the former aristocracy and any opposition political parties. By the 1850's, the United States pressured Spain for the rights to operate military bases to help protect Western Europe from the Soviet Union, and Franco accepted the validity of allowing the bases. With foreign aid, Spain rebuilt rapidly, industrialized and sought to create an atmosphere for tourism and expatriate retirement. Generalisimo Franco became respectable in the eyes of the West despite the brutality of the Spanish Civil War and the way in which he kept opposition groups repressed.

What was most amazing about Franco's rule was the way in which it ended. He chose his successor, which to everyone's surprise was the young Prince Juan Carlos of the House of Bourbon to be restored as the King of Spain. He began grooming the young prince, and most thought that upon Franco's death Spain would be under authoritarian rule from an anointed king. But in 1975 when King Juan Carlos came to the throne, he asked for free elections to the Cortés and set himself at a constitutional monarch rather than becoming an absolute ruler. It was the wisest thing he could have done for himself and the country.

SPAIN TODAY: King Juan Carlos has stepped aside and abdicated the throne to his son King Felipe VI, and the former king now lives in retirement. The Spanish Royal Family has become much loved by the population at large, especially because Juan Carlos brought back democracy, which flourishes.

However, there are problems. The Spanish government has over extended itself and has a massive debt load. Spain, Portugal and Italy are among the three weakest members of the European Union economically, not too far behind Greece, which has suffered economic meltdown. In the early years of entering the European Union in 1986, Spain's economy was booming. Tourism and retirement have played a major role along the Costa del Sol (the southern Mediterranean coast) where posh apartment buildings line the waterfront. But the economic bubble was fueled by more expectation than realization, and now prices have slumped, plunging the country into recession.

In 2004, a terrorist bombing of a Madrid commuter train showed Spaniards that they were vulnerable to Islamic forces within their country. Nearly 200 died and 1,800 were injured in what was one of the most horrific terrorist crimes in Europe. In addition to Islamic terrorists, Spain has continued to have an ongoing war of nerves with the Basque separatists in the north who from time to time do commit acts of terror. In fact the Madrid bombing was first blamed upon the Basque. And more recently the stage for dissolution of the union between the Catalan people and the rest of Spain has surfaced. Barcelona is the major city of Catalonia, which considers its land to be a separate country. Even the act of outlawing bullfighting in Catalonia has shown that the people want to culturally disavow anything Spanish.

BARCELONA:
The grand city of Barcelona, capital of the Province of Catalonia, is Spain's second largest city. Its metropolitan population is 5,375,000, making it the largest urban center along the shores of the Western Mediterranean. Culturally, however, Barcelona is Catalonian, not Spanish, though the Spanish language is widely spoken as a second tongue. For most of us foreign visitors it is hard to see much difference between the two cultural traditions, but believe me they are there and quite visible if you know how to view life in Barcelona.

The expansive harbor of Barcelona makes it Spain's largest seaport. This is officially Spain, but culturally, as noted above, it is not. And what does that exactly mean? Spain is an amalgamation of former kingdoms, having been brought together in the late 15th century by King Ferdinand of Aragon and Queen Isabella of Castille. Barcelona is in the northeastern corner of what is today Spain. It is the chief city and cultural center of Catalonia, a distinctive region that although unified politically with Spain for centuries, it still has culturally maintained its distinctive language, traditions and daily customs. Catalan is a Romanic language that is very similar to Spanish, but yet is distinctive in its own way. Barcelona is essentially a bilingual city with Catalan recognized as the primary language. Recently the province's ban on bullfighting is an example of how they are exercising their cultural rights. In the rest of Spain bullfighting is like a religion. But the Catalonians felt that it was an alien tradition imposed upon them and they exercised their desire to not see it practiced in their territory even though for centuries many Catalonians have supported the sport.

NATURE OF BARCELONA: The city occupies the coastal lowland plain along the northern Mediterranean coast of Spain, only about an hour by car from the French border. High hills back up the city, and Barcelona has grown to the lower base of the hills, but unlike American cities, people here have chosen not to live in the foothills even though they have a sweeping view. The landscape is rather brown and burnt looking during the hot, dry Mediterranean summers. But if a visitor were to come back in winter, the green grasses and wildflowers of the hillsides would be surprising. Winter is the cool, wet season, but only on rare occasions does Barcelona truly have a drastic cold snap.

Barcelona is quite a compact city with the majority of its residents living in apartment blocks. Few single-family homes with gardens are to be found within the immediate urban zone. There are three distinctive parts to the city of Barcelona, each district or zone running parallel to the manmade harbor:
* The Old City that began in medieval times is located close to the waterfront and is comprised of narrow streets with most buildings built out of stone. Here one finds the city's great cathedral and many of the early palatial homes of the wealthy of that period. Streets are narrow and most houses show only a wall with barred windows facing the street, as life is lived in the interior, revolving around the beautiful central courtyard with its fountain.
* Eixample - Extending north along Las Ramblas, the city's grand boulevard that is very pedestrian friendly, the neighborhood becomes more exotic with architecture from the 19th century period of excess and experimentation. This vast region with a regularized grid pattern is known as Eixample. Las Ramblas extends north from the waterfront for several miles. This is the place to be seen, and at all hours of the day its benches are filled with people who sit and simply watch other people or talk and enjoy the fresh air. Lining the street are dozens of cafes, bakeries and shops, adding to the jovial atmosphere.

Eixample is famous for its early 20th century art deco buildings, especially those whimsical ones designed by Antonio Gaudí. I personally find his architecture to be a mix between Disneyland and the Flintstones, but that is only one person's opinion. In the eastern part of Eixample is the masterpiece of Gaudí, the Sagrada Familia. More will follow on the Sagrada Familia.

* Surrounding Eixample on the west, north and east is the newer portion of Barcelona, which consists of more modern buildings. Here one finds apartment complexes, some high-rise office blocks and in the foothills there are single-family homes. The styles vary from traditional Mediterranean similar to what one sees in southern California, to more contemporary structures with a heavy use of glass and sharp angles. From a cultural perspective, this part of the city begins to resemble other cities within the Mediterranean and looses its distinctive architectural charm.

Given that many cruises begin or end in Barcelona, if this is the case for your cruise, then you should plan at least two full days in this amazing city where there is so much to see. If your cruise is simply stopping for one day, then I highly recommend one of your cruise line's half day or all day tours. This is a large city and a bit difficult to see on your own in a single day. As much as I do not favor tours, I recommend one in this instance.

SIGHTS TO SEE: The major highlights to be seen in Barcelona tend to be concentrated in the central portion of the city. There is a Metro, but I do recommend against using it if you are carrying a camera, map or other item that identifies you as a tourist. Pickpockets and muggers do often wait to prey upon tourists in the Metro. You are best off taking a taxi unless you have arranged private cars and drivers. Here are the classic sights nobody should miss:

* Sagrada Familia - This is a massive cathedral that began to be constructed in 1882 and is expected to be completed in 2026 to celebrate the birth of its controversial architect, Antonio Gaudi. The Sagrada Familia is like no other cathedral, built in a combination of Gothic and Art Nouveau styles. It is a fantasy of one man that is at first hard to interpret. Once again my reaction, apart from marveling at its size and the sheer amount of workmanship, was one of seeing this as a piece of architecture that would not be comfortable to live with. If I had to describe the building, I would say that it looks like a collection of large candles that have melted down and the wax is jumbled together. I know I am not being fair in my assessment, but I still feel that a major cathedral needs to have a traditional appearance. Generally as an author I do not interject my personal opinion, but such is the nature of the Sagrada Familia that it engenders personalized commentary. UNESCO has extended World Heritage status to the cathedral. If you are going to visit on your own, the easiest way to get from the cruise ship terminal is by taxi. If you

are staying in the city, some hotels are within walking distance while others are not. Ask your concierge about getting to the cathedral.

* Gothic Quarter or Old City - Extending east and west of Las Ramblas, the Gothic Quarter of the city is filled with crooked, narrow streets that are lined with historic old buildings dating back to what we generally call the Middle Ages.

* Basilica Santa Maria del Mar - The most magnificent of buildings is the Basilica Santa Maria del Mar, which is a grand example of traditional Gothic architecture. This is the heart of the old city and can be reached from the cruise terminal on foot or by taxi. And from hotels, most people will take a taxi.

* Barcelona Cathedra - This is the more traditional Gothic cathedral in the heart of the Old City. It is a magnificent structure not to be missed even for just a few moments worth of standing in awe of its interior.

* Palau de la Musica Orfeo Catalana - Located at 4-6 La Ribera in the city center, this is a magnificent Baroque theater like no other. It is architecturally unique and you should see its magnificent interior. It is open from 9 AM to 9 PM daily except when performances are being held. At those times you do need tickets, but it is well worth the money if you can attend an actual performance.

* Gaudi Architecture - Antonio Gaudi was a unique architect, designing a number of apartment and commercial buildings like no other to be found anywhere in the world. The best way to see examples of his architecture if you are only here for one day on a cruise is to take one of the ship tours that will include at least one or two Gaudi sites. If you are staying in a hotel for a couple of days, then ask about a Gaudi tour, either by coach or on foot depending upon your location. If you cannot arrange any such tour, then at least visit the Casa Batllo on Passeig de Gracia, number 43. The house is open from 9 AM to 9 PM and guided tours are given.

* Mercato Boqueria - Along Las Ramblas is one of the most incredible marketplaces I have ever visited. It is the Mercato Boqueria, a vast collection of stalls selling the most exquisitely displayed foods I have ever seen. Everything from the vegetables, fruits, breads, meats fish and sweets is so beautiful that it is a feast for the eyes, let alone the palate. The marketplace simply dazzles the senses and reflects the gourmet quality of Barcelona. Of all the foods on display, the variety of candy, dried fruits and nuts was like nothing I have ever seen. Every possible variety of these temptations was on display and it was breathtaking, if that can be said about food items.

* Museu Nacional d'Art de Catalunya - The city's magnificent museum housing a major sampling of the art of the region is located near the city center. It fronts on the Montjuic Park in the western part of the city. It is open from 10 AM to 7 PM daily. Once again it is best to reach the museum by taxi because of its location.

* Montjuic Park - If you are going to or coming from the Museu Nacional d'Art Catalunya, you can have your driver take you through Montjuic Park where you will be able to stop and get some dramatic overview photographs of the city. And you can also drive by the Olympic Stadium that was home to the 1992 summer Olympic games. This is one destination where you go on a group tour, have a private car and driver or take a taxi to visit because of its remote location.

* Parc de la Ciutadella - On the east side of the Gothic Quarter, this 18-hectare or 44 acre park is one of the most beautiful in Barcelona. Within the park is the Castell deis Tres Dragons, the Umbracle, which is a large plant greenhouse and the Hivemacle, a large glass house. The very imposing Parliament of Catalunya is located in the heart of the park. You can easily reach the park on foot if your hotel in adjacent to the Gothic Quarter or by taxi from other major hotels.

* Placa d"Espanya - In the western city just north of Montjuic is one of the most strikingly beautiful roundabouts where two grand boulevards cross. This is an excellent area in which to walk just to explore this sector of the city that is filled with many excellent shops, cafes and small museums. This beautiful area of the city can be reached on any number of bus lines if you wish to try local transport. Check with your hotel concierge. If you are on a one-day tour, chances are that at some point in the day your coach will drive through the plaza.

* Tibidabo - Located atop a mountain outside of the city center, Tibidabo consists of a breathtakingly beautiful gothic-style church known as Templo del Sagrado Corazon de Jesus, a vast parkland and an amusement park for children, all with a dramatic view of the city. But you should only plan to visit on an absolutely clear day.

* Park Guell - This is a unique park that once again is a showcase for the world famous architect Antonio Gaudi. It was opened in 1926, and is today one of city's showpieces, also holding UNESCO World Heritage Site status. The park overlooks the city being situated slightly above the median elevation. As you walk along its many paths amid lush greenery, you will see fanciful sculptures, fountains and other constructs all with that specific Gaudi touch, The park is open daily from 8:30 AM to 6:15 PM and can be reached from the center of the city most easily by taxi. Taking the Metro or a city bus is not that convenient, as you will have to walk 25 minutes from the nearest Metro station or anywhere from five to 20 minutes from the four city bus lines that come relatively close. The tourist bus, what is thought of in most cities, as hop on hop off still will only bring you to within a 10 to 15 minute walk to the main entrance.

There are many more sights within Barcelona, but what I have listed are the absolute must see venues, especially if your time in the city is limited. Most cruise passengers generally spend only one day either at the start or conclusion of their cruise. If Barcelona is your point of origin or termination, I highly recommend at least two to three days if you can afford the time.

The city has many outstanding hotels, but check with your cruise line, as they often contract for special rates for guests either embarking or disembarking in Barcelona. And the quality of the hotel will be determined by the quality of the cruise line. If you are a member of the major chains such as Marriott, Hilton, Radisson or Hyatt, check with their office to see what arrangements they are able to make for you.

DINING IN BARCELONA: The city of Barcelona literally has hundreds of restaurants in a wide range of categories. But since this is Spain, I am only recommending restaurants that serve traditional Catalan or Spanish cuisine. I have divided the listing into two sub categories. For those of you whose ship is simply stopping for the day, I have chosen a few outstanding traditional restaurants for lunch. And the second category of restaurant listings is open for dinner, which in Spain is quite late at night. But most restaurants do serve lunch until around 4 PM.
 LUNCH:
* **Restaurant Montiel** - Located on Calle Flassaders 19 and open from 1 to 2:30 PM for Lunch and again from 6:30 to 10:30 PM for dinner. This is a very traditional restaurant specializing in traditional Spanish cuisine. The meals are served in a leisurely manner and are relatively expensive. Advanced reservations are necessary.
* **Can Valles** - Located at Carrer d'Arago 95 between Calabria and Rocafort, open from 1:30 to 4 PM for lunch and 9 to 11 PM for dinner. This is another very traditional restaurant with gourmet Spanish food, but emphasizing meat as a major entree. Reservations are recommended.
* **Informal** - On Calle de la Plata 4 inside Hotel Serras, this restaurant is open from 8 AM to 11 PM serving all three major meals. It is informal as its name implies, reasonably priced and offers a diverse menu but in keeping with Spanish traditions. Reservations are recommended at lunch or dinner.
 DINNER:
* **Blavis** - Located on Carrer Saragossa 85, open from 8 to 11 PM and reservations are a must. This is a small restaurant known for its innovative and beautiful menu for full meals or tapas. This restaurant is expensive, but well worth the price and it is highly sought after so do not try to show up with a reservation.
* **Santa Rita Experience** - This innovative gourmet restaurant with a traditional Spanish menu also requires advanced reservations. It is located on Carrer de Almogaveres 56 and is a very popular favorite with locals.

* Tast Ller - Located at D'Obradors 15 Loft, this is another very popular and highly rated restaurant where a reservation is a must. Dinner is served from 8 to 10 PM, and is a very leisurely experience.
* Viana Barcelona - At Calle Vidre 7 and open from 6 PM to 2:30 AM, this is a beautiful taste experience that captivates. They have a diverse traditional menu that will delight even the fussiest eater. Reservations are a definite must.

SHOPPING IN BARCELONA: This is a large and sophisticated city, and you will find the quality of shopping comparable to other major western European cities. For specific Spanish made crafts or clothing, there are shops that specialize in locally made items, but I do not feel comfortable recommending any particular one since there is such a diversity. Here are my four major recommendations for overall shopping in Barcelona:
* El Corte Ingles - Located on Placa de Catalunya and also Avenida Diagonal 471-73, this is the largest and most famous department store chain in the country. There are branch stores in all major Spanish cities. The two in Barcelona are quite large and have many floors of diverse merchandise. And they do have a department selling typical souvenir items.
* Las Arenas Shopping Mall - Located on Placa d'Espanya, this mall from the outside resembles a large, brick bullfighting arena. Well that is exactly what it once was. But today it is one of the city's most fashionable high-end malls that is well worth a visit for any serious shopper.
* Las Ramblas - Along the city's great boulevard you will find hundreds of shops in all price ranges selling brand merchandise along with locally made handcrafts and clothing. It is simply a matter of browsing and window-shopping until you find a shop that meets your specific needs.
* Portal de l'Angel - This is a small shopping street located very close to Placa Catalunya that offers very special high-end shops with a nice array of merchandise.

Map of the layout of Barcelona (© OpenStreetMap contributors)

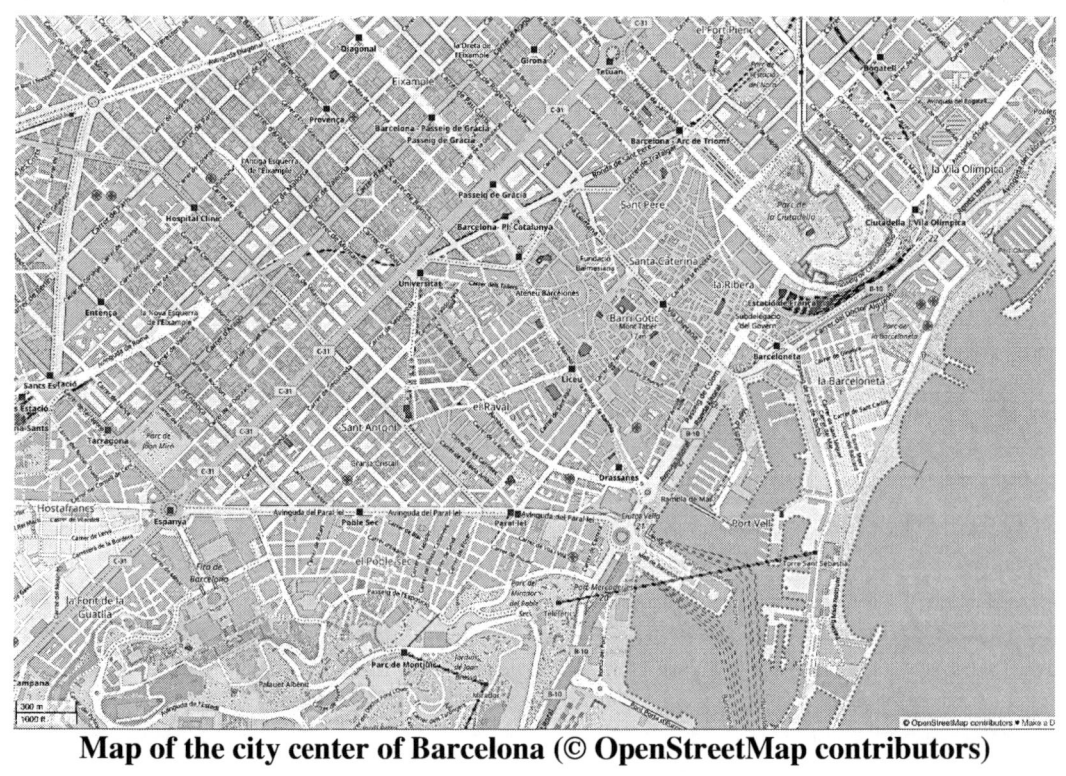

Map of the city center of Barcelona (© OpenStreetMap contributors)

A view over the center of Barcelona from Montjuic

A view over the mid town portion of Barcelona from Mountjuic

A closer view of midtown Barcelona from Montjuic

The medieval Cathedral of Barcelona in the Old City

The Sagrada Familia in Barcelona

The many layers of detail on the facade of the Sagrada Familia

A dramatic view of the Sagrada Familia from Plaza de Gaudi

An example of Gaudi architecture in Barcelona

Plaza Catalunya in the heart of Barcelona

In the Mercato Boqueira of Barcelona

Produce in the Mercato Boqueira of Barcelona

The Mercato Boqueria has no equal in Europe

The Mercato Boqueria is a feast for the senses

VALÈNCIA: The city of València on the Costa Brava or east coast of Spain is one of the country's most notable cities. It has played a major role in the history of the country, and it is also one of the most sought after destinations both for its architecture (both historic and ultra modern) and for its seaside location offering beautiful beaches. The surrounding countryside is also very productive and typifies the agricultural and horticultural diversity of the Mediterranean.

The city of València sprawls along both banks of the Turia River where it empties into the Gulf of València. The city began on what was once an island in the river back in Roman times, but eventually the land was filled in and today the major portion of the urban area, and the city center are both north of the river. To the south of the city around 11 kilometers or 6 miles is the Albufera, a freshwater lagoon in the middle of a vast marshland that provides for recreation and offers a home to waterfowl. The site is now protected and remains in a natural state.

The landscape of the surrounding countryside is gently rolling and slowly leads toward the mountains to the west of the coastal lowlands. This is a highly productive area, and València has been famous for its orange groves, olives, nuts and a variety of fruits along with vines for the production of wine. But today the city is also a major manufacturing and commercial center in addition to it being the hub of a vast agricultural region. Climatically this is typically a Mediterranean region with hot, dry summers and cool and moist winters. But as one travels inland, the landscape becomes more semi arid in the central plateau region of the Iberian Peninsula.

València is Spain's third largest city after Madrid and Barcelona. The population within the metropolitan region is 1,700,000 and growing rapidly. But this is a city with a long history and has much in the way of historic architecture to validate its long tenure. This makes it a city that is high on the visitor's list of places to see in Spain, and a stop in València by cruise ship offers a chance to start becoming familiar with this grand city.

A BRIEF VALÈNCIA HISTORY: You cannot begin to appreciate what you see in València without first knowing the history of this illustrious Spanish city. As this is an information book for potential cruisers, the history is herein presented in as brief a format as is possible without it loosing its vitality.

València dates to 138 BCE, when it was founded as a typical Roman city complete with many public buildings and a forum. It had two main streets that formed the cross around which the city developed. Today the two principal boulevards Calle de Salvador Almoina and Calle de los Caballeros follow the route of those long ago Roman streets. During its long Roman history, it was once destroyed by Pompey in 75 BCE because it had supported Sertorius, Pompey's main rival. It was later rebuilt and again became one of the most beautiful Roman cities in Iberia. But after the fall of Rome, the city declined, however, it remained home to a Christian enclave during the fourth century.

The Byzantine Empire did briefly hold the city between 554 and 625 AD, but lost control when the Visigoths (Germanic invaders) conquered this part of Spain. It was fortified, but there are few historic references to how important or minor the city was to these northern invaders.

When the Moors invaded Spain in 714, the city ultimately began to take on new life when the son of the Emir of Cordoba took over control and built an elegant palace for himself just outside what was then the city. But unfortunately unlike other Spanish cities, no trace remains. Over the next few centuries, València became prosperous as a center for the production of fine quality leather goods, ceramics, glass and metal works. The remains of the city walls, the baths, the minaret of the mosque and several other prominent buildings can still be seen. But unlike Granada, the amount of architecture is far less significant in València.

Like many cities in the Moorish world, València had its ups and downs, as political control waxed and waned. But by the 11th century, the last Taif or kingdom of València saw the construction of a new city wall and numerous other buildings, the remains of which can still be seen today.

The most colorful period of Moorish history occurs between 1092 and 1099, when a Castilian noble, known to us as El Cid, captured the city to create his own mini kingdom, first laying siege to the city for 18-months before it fell. He ruled as a Christian noble and converted many mosques into churches. When the Almoravid Armies laid siege to dislodge El Cid, he fought heroically, but was slain in battle. However, his wife managed to continue to rule for two years following his death, backed by his Christian army, which was able to hold off the Almoravids until 1102. There is a famous Hollywood movie portraying in vivid terms the life of this famous Spaniard. Charlton Heston and Sophia Loren were the two blockbuster stars in this 1961 production.

In real historic terms, the Almoravids briefly held the city but were driven out by Alfonso VI of León and Castile, but the Moors took it back in 1109, but not before Alfonso burned most of it to the ground. The North African Berber Muslims took the city in 1171, and ruled for over 100 years.

In 1238, King James of Aragon conquered the city, bringing to an end Islamic control of València. The Muslims were not driven out of the city but rather allowed to remain if they agreed to certain conditions regarding their loyalty to the new Spanish kingdom. The city now entered its Spanish historic period, which would drastically alter its physical appearance and way of life. Although King James promised equal treatment for Muslims and Jews just as the Moors had given to Christians and Jews, all was not that harmonious. By the middle of the 14th century, plagues and disease in general along with internal warfare among the Christian kingdoms of Spain caused the city to decline. The city became divided into three distinct ethnic neighborhoods and attacks upon Jews and Muslims did occur.

During the 15th century, València did recover its position as an important producer of textiles, ceramics and glass, and trade was brisk. The city grew once again and at one point was the largest city of the Kingdom of Aragon. Even after the Reconquista had swept the Moors from Granada, the last of Islamic kingdoms in Iberia, Muslims in València continued to thrive along with the city's Jewish quarter. By 1502, València even had a university, and the arts along with literature flourished, making this one of the great cities of the Mediterranean well into the 16th century. But the city did loose out on trade with the Americas because of royal prohibitions preventing Mediterranean ports doing direct business with the new American colonies. This did cause a revolt within the guilds of València that was put down with a fair loss of life and hundreds of later executions.

During the early 1600's, the government forced Jews and Muslim descendants who had converted to Christianity to leave València, forcing them to flee to North Africa. This had very strong impact upon many of the nobles of the city who had invested in Jewish and Muslim business ventures.

During the War of Spanish Succession between 1702 and 1709, King Philip V punished the Kingdom of València because the city had supported the Austrians in the succession. It lost most of its political independence. It was forced to conform to the laws governing a more united Spain.

The city once again rose to prominence during the 18th century, as many parts of Spain began to industrialize. The city also once again resumed its role as an important contributor to the arts and literature as well as the sciences, being what they were at that time.

During the Napoleonic invasion of Spain and Portugal, the people of València took up arms against the advancing forces, which they managed to thwart on two occasions. But in October 1811, the city came under siege and bombardment, forcing its surrender in January 1812. The French then ultimately made València the capital of their conquest, and Joseph Bonaparte, the brother of Napoleon became the supposed ruler of Spain. Upon the defeat of Napoleon, the rightful King Ferdinand VII returned to Spain, but he refused to accept a new Constitution that had been drafted by the Cortes convened in Cádiz. The King took up temporary residence in València until his military forces were strong enough and then he returned to Madrid.

During the period following the return of the King up until 1833, the government and Church maintained a firm hand and was very repressive of any individuals or groups who wanted to see more sharing of power rather than absolute rule on the part of the monarch. After the death of Ferdinand VII, the country was in a state of chaos between the forces wanting a more inclusive government and liberalism and those wanting to maintain the old order. In València life continued to surprisingly flourish, but there were many clashes between the two forces throughout the reign of Isabella II who ruled until 1868. The city did see improvements in its infrastructure, expansion of the port and many other urban improvements. Parts of the old city wall were destroyed to allow for urban improvements, but fortunately many sections remained.

During the brief period of Republic during the 1870's, València was once again bombarded and suffered much damage. But even with the restoration of the Bourbon crown, the city remained a hot bed of liberal thinking. As the city expanded and the economy grew, the planting of orange groves and vineyards added to the overall wealth of the landed class, and also brought more trade through the city's port. Although during World War I, exports of citrus, grapes, wine and other agricultural products was greatly hampered, causing a major decline in the overall prosperity of València. And during the Spanish Civil War, the city had been a stronghold for those opposed to the Franco forces, and once again it was bombarded and suffered significant damage.

Since the start of the 20th century, València has maintained its position as both the third largest city in Spain and the third most important economically. The role of tourism actually came late apart from those Europeans and other foreigners who would make brief visits to marvel at the city's beautiful examples of traditional Spanish architecture. The city has always been subjected to period flash floods on the Turia River, but in 1949 and again in 1957, the level of flooding was quite dramatic. And the true loss of life has never been fully agreed upon. Ultimately the river was diverted to flow farther south of the city to prevent future flooding. And the old riverbed is today a beautiful parkland that skirts along the eastern edge of the old city center.

In the past three decades, València has become one of the most famous cities in the world for many of its exceptionally modern buildings, the work of several now acclaimed architects.

The role of the beach and of expatriate retirement, which so dominates coastal Spain today, did not really begin to flourish until the decade following the end of World War II.

SIGHTS TO SEE: On a one-day port call it will be impossible to see more than a fraction of the traditional and modern architecture of València or to even begin to grasp the flavor of this magnificent city. My suggestion is to take one of the city tours offered by your cruise line simply because it will be next to impossible to get around fast enough on your own to gain a true impression of the city. The ideal scenario is of course to have a car and driver, but for many the cost is beyond what their budget will permit. And to attempt to rent a car and drive around on your own would be futile. I will present what I believe are the most important venues to be visited, but depending upon the types of tours your cruise line provides, you may or may not see all or a large part of the sites listed. But whatever you will see will be impressive and give you somewhat of a picture of València and no doubt entice you to return on your own.

The major must see venues in València are:
* València Cathedral - This is a truly magnificent structure that was begun in 1262 on the site of what is believed to have been the Roman Temple of Diana and later the Moorish Mosque. But the cathedral is of totally Gothic origin. Its distinctive bell tower stands over 58 meters or 190 feet high. The cathedral's dome was added during the 17th century and is of Baroque design. The cathedral is open from 8 AM to 8 PM daily and is in the heart of the Old City.
* Old City of València and it contains a maze of crooked and narrow streets with buildings dating back to Moorish times along with the many centuries of Spanish construction. There are many individual sites within the Old City that are of specific interest such as the cathedral noted above.
* Mercado Central - This is the largest public food market in Europe, and the building dates back to the early 20th century and has a distinctive Art Nouveau style, making it quite worth visiting. It is located in the Old City on the Plaza del Mercado 6.
* La Lonja de la Seda is the old silk market building that was constructed in the 14th century when the production of silk was a major fact of life in València. Today it is open to the public, and architecturally it is quite a distinctive and elegant piece of architecture. It is located on the Plaza del Mercado across from the Mercado Central.

* Antiguo Cauce del Rio Turia is the beautiful park that gracefully curves through the heart of the city, once having been the channel of the river before the 1957 flood. Today it is a grand and wonderful parkland with walking and bicycle trails, fountains, small lakes and lush vegetation. Many visitors exclaim that they only wish their city had such a park.
* Ciutat de les Arts i les Ciències is a masterpiece of ultra modern artistic achievement. Apart from being a series of museums devoted to arts, science, oceanography, musical performances and an IMAX theater along with indoor parking, this is a futuristic vision of what cities in the 22nd or 23 centuries may look like. It is the pride and joy of the city. Located at Avenida del Profesor Lopez Pinero 7, it is open daily from 10 AM to 6 PM and is on almost all group tour itineraries.
* Palacio del Marques de Dos Aguas was once a noble palace of grand acclaim. Today it serves as an art museum that features the ceramic history of València, but apart from its function, the building itself gives you an idea of the golden years of the city's power.
* Plaza de la Virgen is one of the most beautiful squares in the Old City adjacent to the Cathedral de València. It is a place of calm and antiquity, a place to enjoy its tranquil waters and to people watch.

There are many other scenic and historic venues around the city of València, but the one day port call will not give you much time to do more than what I have listed above even with a private car and driver. If you choose one of the ship tours, it may be possible that a given itinerary might include one of the historic small towns outside of the city. And there are just too many external sights to comfortably list in this chapter.

DINING OUT: the majority of you will no doubt be on a tour of València offered by your cruise line. And most tours of greater than six hours duration will include a group lunch at a restaurant chosen by the company. For those of you who will be on your own, I am listing a few choice restaurants in the central part of the city that offer quality and tradition with regard to typical Spanish cuisine.

My choices for restaurants include:
* E; Temple - Located in the city center at Los Centelles 37 and open from Noon to 4 PM for lunch is a very traditional Spanish restaurant that also serves a broad selection of tapas as well as full meals.
* Navarro - Located at Calle Arzobispo Mayoral 5 in the city center, but very popular so it is best to book a table in advance. It is known for its seafood paella, which is about as traditional as one can get in Spain.

* El Bouet - In the city center at Calle Puerto Rico 36, and once again very traditional Spanish and overall Mediterranean cuisine being served in a comfortable atmosphere. It would be wise to book in advance.
* El Celler de Tossal - In the city center on Calle Quart 2, and only open from 2 to 4 PM for lunch, this is an excellent restaurant with a menu that features many meat dishes along with fresh seafood, all beautifully prepared.

SHOPPING: As in all major Spanish cities, València has its large department stores and a wide array of high-end specialty shops. But for visitors who might be looking for souvenirs or Spanish craft items, your best chance will be in the Old City where more tourists visit than locals.

CARTAGENA: Not all cruise itineraries include this very old and historic Spanish port city on the southern coast. But as the years progress, it is becoming more important as a cruise ship stop because of its historic flavor. More people from the Americans are familiar with Cartagena de los Indies in Colombia than the city it is named after in Spain.

Cartagena is located in one of the few lowland coastal regions of Spain known as Campo de Cartagena. The city is an important port because of its rather narrow channel that is squeezed in between several jagged hills that rise up on either side of the harbor mouth. The old city is built at the head of the waterway and then new Cartagena spreads out to the north and northwest. The site was easily defended in the days when warfare dominated the region's history. It was next to impossible for an enemy ship to approach Cartagena without coming under withering crossfire from fortresses perched on the hills to the east and west of the harbor. The city has a population of just over 219,000 residents and serves a hinterland with a total populating, including the city, of just over 400,000 people.

The climate of Cartagena is typical of the Mediterranean coast with mild and moist winters and warm to hot and dry summers. But the city has not developed a major tourist industry because it lacks the extensive beaches that are so vital to the Costa del Sol's tourist industry.

A BRIEF CARTAGENA HISTORY: The city of Cartagena has a history that extends back over two millennia, making it one of Spain's most historic cities. The city's origins can be traced to the Carthaginians at about 227 BCE. The name of the city is actually a corruption of the original name Qart Hadasht, which was the name of ancient Carthage. The city also became an important regional center once Rome had conquered southern Spain, as evidenced by

Roman ruins still found in the urban area. The Roman theater in Cartagena is the second largest in all of Spain and Portugal.

During the Moorish period of occupying southern Spain, Cartagena was of far less significance than many other cities in the south, but was still a somewhat significant port.

Once the Reconquista was complete and the Spanish kingdom came into being, it became one of the most major military ports in all of southern Spain because of its defensible harbor. By the mid 18th century, Cartagena had become the major center for the Spanish Navy's Mediterranean fleet. And today it still holds the role of being one of the country's most prominent naval centers. Because of its late 19th and early 20th century prominence as a port, Cartagena has many fine examples of Art Nouveau architecture, which became quite the style popular in the more affluent Mediterranean cities.

SIGHTS TO SEE: The easiest way to see the sights of Cartagena is to take one of the tours offered by your cruise line or to have the ship's personnel arrange for a private car and driver. Since the port is adjacent to the old heart of the city, it will be easy to walk and see many of the historic sites, but some of the important forts and vantage points are well beyond what is feasible by walking. Local taxi services are available, but often the drivers speak little or no English. The most important sites that should be seen include:

* Bateria de Castellitos - Located atop a rocky promontory overlooking the city, the Bateria de Castellitos presents a mighty fortress replete with huge canons that were able to totally protect the harbor from invasion. It is necessary to take a taxi to reach this hilltop fortress unless you are on a group or private tour.
* The Roman Theater and Museum - Here is one of the finest examples of a large Roman amphitheater with its own museum filled with Roman artifacts dating back almost 2,000 years. The theater is located in the old city center at Plaza Condesa de Peralta.
* Museo Naval - This is the naval museum that traces the history of the Spanish Navy as seen through the port of Cartagena. It is located along Calle Menendez Palayo 6 just west of the city center and open daily.
* Conception Castle - Built in the 12th century, this medieval castle overlooks the city and offers close in views of Old Cartagena. It also has an excellent collection of artifacts dating back to prehistoric, Greek, Phoenician, Roman and Spanish medieval times. The castle is located in Parque Torres Monte de la Concepcion and is open daily.
* Bario del Foro Romano - Located in the Casco Antiguo part of the city on Cale Honda, this is the old center of the Roman city, what is known as the

Forum. It is well preserved and gives a good look at life in this onetime Roman outpost.

* Museo Nacional de Arqueologia Subacuatica - This museum located along Paseo Alfonso XII 22 is along the main waterfront, and it is devoted to the archaeological treasures brought up from the Atlantic representing prehistoric culture in the region.

* Palacio Consistorial - This most beautiful 19th century building serves as the city hall for Cartagena, and it is also a museum telling the city's history. It is located on the main Plaza del Ayuntamiento.

* Spanish Civil War Museum - Located in the city center at Calle Gisbert, and telling the story of the brutal events of the Spanish Civil War from 1936 to 1939.

There are many more sites to see in and around Cartagena, but if you are out on your own, the listings above will easily fill up your day. And most of the tours of the city will include these major sites. To range farther out of the city in the short time available is difficult unless you sign onto one of the group tours that may be traveling deeper into the interior of the Province of Murica.

DINING OUT: You will only be in Cartagena long enough to enjoy lunch; thus the restaurants I have listed are open and specialize in the afternoon meal, and serving traditional Spanish cuisine. Normally most Spaniards have just an afternoon snack and then partake of a heavy evening meal at around 9 or 10 PM. My select choices for lunch are:

* Casa Beltri - Located on Calle Mesina in the heart of the city and it is open from 1 to 4 PM daily for lunch. The cuisine is typically Spanish with a wide variety of dishes from which to choose along with fine accompanying wines. They also offer a tasting menu. And prices are moderate.

* El Encuentro - Located on Principe de Vergara 2 in the city center, this restaurant is known for its high quality Spanish cuisine. One of the signature dishes is paella, which is a very traditional Spanish favorite. The restaurant is open at 11 AM and stays open until 1 AM. Prices are moderate.

* Bodgega la Fuente - Located at Calle Jara 17 in the city center, this restaurant is essentially a tapas bar. If you have not tried tapas and are interested in this Spanish tradition of small dishes served along with your drinks, it is a unique experience and will fill you up the longer you linger.

* Casa Cassciaro - In the city center at Calle del Canon 5, this is another tapas bar where you have many appetizers to choose from, which essentially builds a meal in slow progression. This is very traditional in Spain for afternoon meal or in the early evening before dinner.

SHOPPING: Other than four souvenirs, there is not much to buy in Cartagena that you would not have seen in Barcelona or other major cities.

Most of the major shops are located along the beautiful Calle Mayor, a street that is at the heart of the old inner city. There are plenty of shops to choose from that specialize in objects d'art, leather goods and craft items, but this is not a city where you will find a dazzling array of goods as in Málaga or Barcelona.

A map of greater València (© OpenStreetMap contributors)

A view over the heart of the city from the Cathedral Tower

Old and new architecture of València (Work of Joan Banjo, CC BY SA 3.0, Wikimedia.org)

The famous Torres de Serrans (Work of Dorieo, CC BY SA 3.0, Wikimedia.org)

Old balconies attest to the past flavor of the city, (Work of Joan Banjo, CC BY SA 3.0, Wikimedia.org)

The modern skyline of central València (Work of Joan Banjo, CC BY SA 3.0, Wikimedia.org)

The facade of San Joan del Mercat typifies Old City València (Work of Miguel Hermoso Cuesta, CC BY SA 4.0, Wikimedia.org)

The Cathedral of València (Work of Pere Lopez, CC BY SA 3.0, Wikimedia.org)

The city building of València (Diego Dieso, CC BY SA 4.0, Wikimedia.org)

The Central Market of València (Work of Nicholas Vollmer, CC BY SA 2.0, Wikimedia.org)

The city of Arts and Sciences of València (Work of Balky, CC BY SA 4.0, Wikimedia.org)

A map of greater Cartagena (© OpenStreetMap contributors)

Flying over the center of Cartagena (Work of Phillip Capper, CC BY SA 2.0, Wikimedia.org)

An overview of Cartagena (Work of Martin Stiburek, CC BY SA 4.0, Wikimedia.org)

Looking over the Plaza España (Work of P4K1T0, CC BY SA 4.0, Wikimedia.org)

One of the old fortified walls of Cartagena (Work of Øyvind Holmstad, CC BY SA 4.0, Wikimedia.org)

The ancient Roman amphitheater in Cartagena

The Puerta de Murcia (Work of Øyvind Holmstad, CC BY SA 4.0, Wikimedia.org))

The Puerto Marina Amar

The Gran Hotel (Work of Murcianboy, CC BY SA 3.0, Wikimedia.org)

MÁLAGA:

Málaga is in the southern province of Andalusia, a region that has a close affinity to the American Southwest. It was from this part of Spain, which had been dominated for centuries by the Islamic Moors, that many of the settlers came to México and ultimately influenced what is now Arizona, New Mexico and western Texas. Thus the architecture we recognize as Spanish, or some call it Latin American, actually first came from northern Africa, having been introduced into Spain by the Moors. In the coastal regions, red tile became a common roofing material, and that style has infused itself into the architecture of California, and also to some degree coastal Florida, where the Spanish had also colonized.

Many cruise itineraries for the western Mediterranean either begin or terminate in Málaga while others continue on or are coming from Lisbon. If your cruise is either starting or terminating in Málaga, I strongly urge you to remain for a day or two because there is much to see and do in and around the city. If your cruise itinerary is simply stopping for a day in Málaga, there are two options to consider. One is to do a group or private tour of the city for half a day and then simply enjoy walking around the city center or waterfront for the rest of the day. The second option is to take an all day tour to Granada, which was one of the most influential cities during the long Moorish history of southern Spain. Architecturally Granada is quintessential Mediterranean Spain and it has had a major influence on the Spanish architecture seen in Latin America and the American Southwest. It is also a very romantic city, one filled with great charm.

Málaga is the largest city along the famous Costa del Sol with a population of 570,000 and a metro area population of just over 1,000,000. It occupies the narrow river valley of the Rio Guadalamedina and extends up into the hillsides on both sides of the waterway. The city also occupies the very narrow coastal strip that parallels the Mediterranean. More of the city lies within the hills than on the level coastal plain or river valley, however those areas have very high-density apartment blocks with many classed as high-rise.

The climate is typically Mediterranean with very cool and wet winters still interspersed with long sunny periods. But summer days are relatively hot and dry, rain being quite rare. However, cooling breezes do blow in off the sea and temper the summer heat. Málaga boasts of having around 300 sunny days per year, and this has made it a very popular tourist destination and home to thousands of retired expatriates who love the sun, sand and sea. Málaga is the central city of Spain's popular Costa del Sol.

As a major city, Málaga has excellent transport services with it being the junction of the coastal and interior expressways, a focal railway center and it also does have limited international air services.

A BRIEF MÁLAGA HISTORY: Málaga has a long and fascinating history that has left its mark with many important and beautiful landmarks in and around the city center.

Its history begins approximately 770 BCE when the Phoenicians first settled along the coast. Next in succession came dominance by the ancient city of Carthage, which is relatively close across this narrow part of the sea. North Africa is only approximately 140 kilometers or 80 miles from Málaga and Carthage once dominated this entire coastal region.

By 218 BCE, Rome had conquered Carthage and much of southern Spain, placing the city under its rule. And as master builders, the Romans left behind numerous examples of their architecture, especially a magnificent amphitheater right in the center of the city. After Rome fell, the Visigoths and Byzantium briefly occupied this part of Spain.

The longest period of history before the Reconquista was that of the Moors who occupied Málaga and the rest of southern Spain for 800 years. But the Moorish period was one of turmoil and the actual rule over the city passed through several caliphates and emirates. In its last period of occupancy, Málaga fell under the rule of Granada. It was highly prized as a port and for the extensive agriculture found in the valleys north of the city - citrus, vineyards and fruit orchards. It finally fell to Christian soldiers in 1487 just ahead of the total collapse of Muslim rule in 1492. The city therefore shows a great mix of architectural styles that span nearly three millennia, making it one of the oldest cities of Europe.

From a cultural perspective, Málaga has been the birthplace of several greats, namely film star Antonio Banderas and Pablo Picasso. The city was also the inspiration for the piano or orchestral composition called Malagueña, a piece that evokes images of flamenco, bullfighting and Spanish doñas with their mantillas among other evocative pictures.

During the long Spanish history of the city, the most important military action that Málaga saw as the naval Battle of Málaga, which took place out at sea in 1704, part of the conflict earlier noted as the War of the Spanish Succession where several nations fought over which royal house would rule Spain.

During the Spanish Civil War Málaga was the home base for the Spanish Republican Navy and its port and waterfront were heavily damaged when the Nationalist forces bombarded the city. Generalisimo Franco's forces captured the city in 1937, and then killed many Republican supporters. Later Republican Navy ships again shelled the city in an attempt to dislodge the Nationalists.

Surprisingly under the Franco regime, Málaga began to develop along with the rest of the Costa del Sol as Spain's premier resort area. This was part of Franco's overall plan to improve the economic conditions of the country. And since the return of the monarchy, as a constitutional government, the Costa del Sol has been one of Spain's shining examples of modern development.

SIGHTS TO SEE: Málaga is a city where you can spend the entire day if you are only visiting on a port call, or you can linger for several days if your cruise is either starting or terminating here. And then there is Granada, which is one of the most beautiful cities in all of Spain. Those of you who are spending a few days in Málaga should absolutely not miss Granada. For those here only on a port call, it is hard to recommend either Granada or Málaga for your day's sightseeing. I must leave it up to you, as I have been to both cities and find them equally romantic, historic and enjoyable. If really pressed for a decision, as one who has always been so fascinated by what the Moors did contribute to the overall Spanish culture, I would have to choose Granada. So you decide what you want to do for your one day in port. I will have an additional section that follows in which I will describe Granada.

Here are my recommendations for what to see in Málaga:
* Alcazaba - Overlooking the city center is the imposing stone fortress known as Alcazaba. Built between 1057 and 1063, this is a classic example of the intent of the Moors to fortify their position and remain in Spain. This is the best-preserved Moorish fortification in Spain. The view over the city alone is worth the visit, as are the elegantly manicured gardens.
* Castillo de Gibralfaro - Also sitting on top of a high promontory with a commanding view of the city is the Castillo de Gibalfaro. If you are on your own and not part of a tour, take a taxi, as the climb to the top if for those who are young and in good physical shape. There has been a fortification on this site since the days of the Phoenicians. The Kingdom of Granada at the start of the 14th century built the fortress castle, and it sits within the earlier perimeter of the Phoenician fortification.
* Málaga Cathedral - This impressive Baroque cathedral dominates the older part of the city center. It has a massive main church and two equally impressive side chapels, and is home to the Bishop of Málaga who presides over its more important masses. The church is open daily except Sunday when

it is at its most crowded. If you come during a mass, please be respectful. Women must have their shoulders and heads covered before entering the main sanctuary.

* **Paseo del Parque** - Fronting on the marina and located below the Alcazaba, this magnificent and grand park is the cornerstone of the city center. With fountains, flowerbeds and quiet paths, it is a lovely place to just relax and soak in the scenery.

* **Plaza de la Constitucion** - The main plaza of the city, it is a place to just sit and soak up some sun and people watch. There are beautiful examples of Málaga architecture surrounding the plaza, and also several outdoor cafes that front on the square. It is the spiritual heart of the city and should be visited.

* **Mercado Central de Ataranzas** - Here is the most colorful of the city's marketplaces where you will see a wide variety of the produce, seafood, cheeses, breads, meats and fish from the surrounding countryside. It is enjoyable just to stroll through the market, and if you ask politely, you can sample some of the foods being offered. It is located on Calle Ataranzas 10 in the city center.

* **Museo Picasso Málaga** - If you appreciate the artistry of Pablo Picasso, then this is a must see venue. If you do not care for his work, then by all means this is not a place to visit. The museum is located in Palacio de Buenavista San Agustin 8 in the city center and opens daily at 10 AM.

* **Cac Málaga Centro de Arte Contemporaneo de Málaga** - This is a free museum located on Calle Alemania alongside the river, and open daily at 10 AM. But like the Picasso Museum, you must be one who appreciates modern art otherwise this is not a venue to be visited.

* **Centre Pompidou Málaga** - This is still one more museum of contemporary art, but one housed in a very modern building that is itself worthy of seeing. Located along Pasaje Doctor Carrillo Casssaux across from the Passeo Parque at the east end of the marina. It opens daily at 9:30 AM, but the interior collection is once again only appreciated if you like contemporary art.

* **Playa de la Malagueta** - This is the main beach closest to the city center. It is a bit crowded on warm days, but still a beautiful place for sun, sand and sea.

DINING OUT: If you are visiting Málaga for the day, and you are out on your own, here are my recommendations for lunch in the true Spanish tradition, followed by a few dinner recommendations for those who are staying in the city either before or after their cruise:

LUNCH:

* **El Meson de Cervantes** - No doubt the most popular restaurant for lunch or dinner, located at Calle Alamos 11. Reservations are advised due to the fact that this is one of the most recommended restaurants in the city. The menu is

traditional, the selections limited, but every dish is lovingly prepared and served. You will not be disappointed.

* Sabor a Fuego - At Paseo de Sancha 30, you should book in advance, as this is a popular lunch spot open from 12:30 to 4 PM. And they reopen at 8 PM for dinner. If you are on your own and do not have a private car, you will need to take a taxi, as the restaurant is east of the city center along the main coastal road. Their menu is diverse from stuffed chicken to barbecued meats with a variety of appetizers, soups and salads all in the Spanish tradition.

* La Recova - At Passaje Nuestra Señora de los Dolores de San Juan 5, this restaurant is actually open from 8:30 AM to 4 PM and serves outstanding, traditional Spanish cuisine for breakfast and lunch.

DINNER:

* El Meson de Cervantes - See the listing above under lunch.

* Restaurante Amador - At Calle Bandaneria 6, you will be able to dine on an outdoor terrace or inside and have a superb view of the city. It is open from 8 until 11 PM and a reservation is recommended. The food is considered to be very traditional, but service can be a bit slow, but in the evening most people do not mind. The restaurant prides itself in using fresh quality ingredients and adheres to traditional recipes.

* La Luz de Candela - At Calle Dos Aceras 18020, this is a very traditional Spanish restaurant with outstanding cuisine, featuring both a tapas menu and regular dinner menu with a great range of seasonal dishes. A reservation is recommended. They are open for lunch from 12:30 to 3:30 PM and dinner from 7:30 to 11:30 PM.

SHOPPING: Málaga would be similar to Barcelona when it comes to shopping, having the same major department stores and offering much the same European, imported and some Spanish made merchandise.

* Calle Larios is the main shopping street and it is pedestrian friendly. Here you will find the largest collection of shops in the city center of Málaga.

* Plaza de la Constitucion also offers many traditional shops, some of which will be carrying hand made items of Spanish origin.

There are several major suburban shopping malls, but they will not be offering anything you would not see in other European cities.

GRANADA:
If you are staying in Málaga for just a day as part of your cruise itinerary, it is a hard choice as to see the city or spend the entire day visiting historic and romantic Granada. As I mentioned before, if pushed to make a recommendation, it would have to be Granada, but then you do have to sacrifice Málaga and that is a shame. But if you miss Granada, that is also a shame. Hopefully one cruise line will offer an overnight visit, which

would allow both. But if your cruise begins or terminates in Málaga, then you can arrange to stay over and do both. This would be the ideal situation.

Granada is the city that to me is the heart and soul of Spain. The name has always called up the lyrics of the song of the same name that say, *"Granada I'm falling under your spell, and if you could speak what a fascinating tale you would tell...."* To anyone who lives in the American Southwest or has come from one of the Spanish speaking countries of Latin America, this city represents the glory of Spain with regard to the beautiful architectural legacy it brought to the New World. Granada was the final capital and royal center of the Moors, and it was here that they brought their architectural and landscape styles to fruition, leaving this heritage that is still a part of southern Spain and Latin America, as well as the American Southwest.

Granada is an inland city, about two hours from Málaga via excellent divided highway. The city is located at the base of the nearly 12,000 foot high Sierra Nevada; the mountains whose name was given to California's equally beautiful snow covered peaks. The name actually means mountains of snow. The first time I went was in early May and I did not expect to see much, if any snow on Spain's Sierra Nevada. To my surprise, as I neared Granada, they were draped in a heavy white mantle that just added to the glorious aura of the city itself. The route there will take you through the coastal mountains; past grove after grove of olive trees and small-whitewashed villages that each would have dated back centuries. The drive alone is worth the trip, but then Granada absolutely becomes the icing on the cake, as it lives up to every expectation you might have that dates back to your first historic studies of Spain.

Leaving the express highway, the main road enters Granada through the modern suburbs where blocks of high-rise apartments and small shopping plazas dominate. Slowly the road leads into the central core of the city, which is quite congested, as this is a major university city and regional trade center with a population of over 350,000 people. The overall flavor is Spanish, but lacking the distinctive whitewashed flat roofed style you are expecting. Some of the buildings from the 18th and 19th centuries feature Baroque and art deco styles similar to Barcelona. It is not until crossing the river into the truly old city that everything changed. Old Granada, which is very extensive in size, is where the romantic flavor lies.

Crowning a high hill above the old city is the number one attraction of Granada – The Alhambra. This is the grand palace complex built by the Moorish sultans from which they ruled over their Spanish empire. Granada became the capital of a Berber kingdom in the 11th century, after a civil war among the Islamic ruling families. And it is here that architecture reached a sublime excellence from which all of the elegant elements have been copied and reinterpreted in the architectural heritage of the Spanish-speaking world. Even in Manila, Philippines this heritage can be seen. Thus from California to Colombia to Argentina to Puerto Rico and across the world to the Philippines the influences of the Alhambra palace can be felt. Although distinctly Arabic in flavor, the Alhambra made use of the pitched roof covered in ceramic tile and the open balconies that invite cooling breezes, as after all this is a moderate climate unlike the deserts from where the Moorish ancestry originated.

The Alhambra is not simply one palace, but rather a collection of palaces and gardens spread across the brow of a massive hill. It covers hundreds of manicured acres, the gardens retaining the same qualities and irrigation systems that were established by the Moors. The Royal Family of a united Spain constructed only one Baroque summer palace after the final Reconquista that drove the last of the Moors out of Spain in 1492, but it was never occupied. It stands in total contrast to the beautiful colonnades and arched windows of the Moorish buildings where a filigree of lacy and delicate carvings predominates on balustrades and windows. The designs represent flowers and quotes from the Koran, as in true Islamic fashion the representation of God or Mohammed was never permitted.

Visiting the Alhambra can be the fulfillment of decades of marvel from pictures of this historic complex whose architecture had such a profound impact upon Spain, Latin America and the American Southwest. Only somebody who has studied the history of the American Southwest and who has seen the capital city of New Mexico, Santa Fe and other important local sites can truly have the deep appreciation what the Alhambra and Old Granada represented.

Because the Alhambra is a UNESCO World Heritage Site, the Spanish authorities in charge of its operation and maintenance only allow a certain number of people to enter each day. Thus it is imperative that you go as part of a group or private tour, either from the cruise line, or a reputable company if you are staying over in Málaga either before or after your cruise. If you should rent a car and drive to Granada on your own, there is little chance you will be admitted to the Alhambra.

DINING OUT: Granada has many fine restaurants, but most are open only for dinner. I am recommending a few traditional Spanish restaurants that do serve lunch for those going independently. But if you are on a group tour, lunch is generally included.

My choices for lunch in Granada are:
* Sabor y Saveur - Located at Castillas del Prat 9, this is one of the most highly recommended restaurants serving very traditional food that is typical of the area. It is open from 1 to 4 PM daily for lunch and reservations are recommended. But at slack times when there are fewer visitors in the city, you can be served without a reservation.
* Carmela Restaurante - Located on Calle Colcha 13, and open from 8 AM to Midnight, you have a wide range of times for lunch. Reservations are always advised. The food and service are excellent. There are many traditional seafood and rice dishes, and a wide array of hams and roasted meats. And do not forget dessert.
* Casa Piti - Known for its traditional atmosphere and food, located on Calle del Agua del Albayzin 20, this gem of a restaurant offers excellent service despite its small size, and the cuisine is very traditional to Granada. It is open all afternoon, but a reservation is always best.

SHOPPING: As a major city, the main shopping area once again has all of the important stores you will have seen in Barcelona and Málaga. But as a city filled with history that attracts visitors, there are areas where you can find local crafts such as fine embroidery, leather and other handcrafts. My recommendations are:
* Plaza Bib-Rambla - This is one of the city's central plazas and is in the center of a major shopping and dining area. You will find a lot of small shops, many of them selling handcraft items and also Arabic goods. This is also a nice place for a cup of coffee, chocolate and a chance to munch on some churros.
* Calle Elvira - In the city center at Plaza Mariana Pineda, you will find this narrow street filled with a variety of shops. Many sell goods brought across from North Africa, as they represent similar styles as would have been found in the Moorish days of Granada. There are also plenty of souvenir items, and some finer quality leather goods.
* Calle Navas - Also in the city center, this is a street lined with curio stores, tapas bars and small cafes. It is a good place for souvenir shopping rather than high quality handcrafts.

A map of greater Málaga (© OpenStreetMap contributors)

An overview of Málaga (Work of andrew j w, CC BY SA 2.0, Wikimedia.org)

Arriving in the port of Málaga at sunset

Jardines de Puerta Oscura along the Málaga waterfront

The medieval Málaga Cathedral

Plaza de la Marina at Christmas time

Paseo Molina Lario from Paseo del Parque in the heart of Málaga

Calle Marques de Larios at Christmas time

The ancient Roman amphitheater in the city center

The tranquil beauty of suburban Málaga

A map of the city of Granada (© OpenStreetMap contributors)

A view of the Sierra Nevada upon entering the city of Granada

Overlooking Granada from en route to the Alhambra

A view over the old city portion of Granada from the Alhambra

A second view over the old city of Granada from the Alhambra

In the heart of downtown modern Granada

The Summer Gardens of the Alhambra

The Summer Palace at the Alhambra

The Throne Palace at the Alhambra

The fine quality of the marble carving at the Alhambra

PALMA de MAJORCA: Many cruise ships pay a visit to the beautiful and oh so popular island of Majorca, one of Spain's major tourist destinations. The city of Palma is the largest settlement and capital of the Balearic Islands, which lie in the Mediterranean southeast of Barcelona. Palma is a significant medium size city of just over 402,000 residents, many of them being expatriate retirees from all across Western Europe and even North America. Even the Spanish Royal Family spends many holidays on the island. Dependent upon the length of your cruise and its overall final destination, it may or may not stop at Palma, as not all cruise lines include it in their Western Mediterranean itineraries.

The Balearic Islands are relatively mountainous, especially the four largest islands of Majorca, Menorca, Ibizia and Formentera. The highest mountain peak on Majorca rises up to 1,364 meters or 4,475 feet above sea level. Although not very high, the island is quite rugged and has dramatic sea cliffs along its northern coast. The Balearic Islands are essentially the tops of an uplifted platform and not volcanic activity, which is unlike Spain's Canary Islands. Climatically the islands are very mild because of their small size and the cooling sea breezes that penetrate even into the interior. They have cool, moist winters and mild to moderately warm, but dry summers. Today because of the heavy pressure brought about by a high population, the number of hotels, swimming pools and golf courses, the island water table has dropped dramatically. During the dry summers, water must be brought from the mainland by tankers to augment the local supply. And desalinization is also being used. Once these islands were known for their fruit orchards and vineyards, but that is constantly being sacrificed for urbanization.

A BRIEF HISTORY: The Roman elite loved the seclusion and tranquility of small islands, as witnessed by the popularity of Capri off of Naples. Palma was founded by Rome in 123 BCE, and the main purpose was as a supply and naval center for later Roman occupation of Carthage and the south of Spain. Unfortunately there are no significant ruins to attest to the Roman period of Palma.

After the fall of the Roman Empire, the island of Majorca did see some Byzantine settlement, but again little remains to give a clear picture as to the significance of the eastern empire having truly been established here. But the history of the island is well documented from 707 to 1229 AD during the Moorish period. The island continued to be totally self supporting with agriculture practiced along with piracy, many of the residents being early Christians from the Roman and Byzantine periods. The Christian pirates preyed upon all who passed, be they Muslim or Christian, and the islanders became relatively wealthy in their isolation. But they did incur retaliation from the Moorish navy on several occasions. And by the mid 9th century, the Caliphate of Córdoba did incorporate the Balearic Islands into its nation. This not only brought a semblance of real government, but it also encouraged legitimate trade and some degree of manufacturing in small workshops.

In the 11th century, as the Córdoba Caliphate was in a state of disarray, the province of the Balearic Islands ultimately broke free and established itself as its own Islamic state. The islands were used for attacks on Christian shipping, especially eastward toward the Italian coast. Despite Pisa and Genoa having become major merchant ports, they were still no equals in engagements with the Moorish raiders. But by 1090, the Christian states had become better organized, and in 1115, Palma was raided and pillaged by forces from Barcelona and Provence. But despite this setback, the Moors still held the island although there was a succession of mainland caliphates that held sway over the islands.

In 1229, Christian forces under James I from Aragon conquered the islands and Palma became the capital of a new Spanish Kingdom of Majorca. Now under Spanish Christian control, many of the beautiful palaces, monasteries and the great cathedral in Palma all began to rise to attest to the importance of the islands as part of the Reconquista.

This golden age did not last too long. As the nobility and merchant classes gained wealth and power, the peasants languished. But in the 16th century there was a major rebellion, which caused a contraction of the upper classes and the Church behind more defensive positions. And ultimately the power and wealth of the islands declined. Palma degenerated into a rather shabby city, one patronized by pirates and privateers and it would not be until late 19th and early 20th century tourism that the prosperity returned. It was in 1833, that the Balearic Islands actually became recognized as a separate province independent of any mainland governments.

SIGHTSEEING IN PALMA: The vast majority of cruise ships that visit the Balearic Islands make Palma de Majorca their port of call. A few smaller cruise ships may stop at the island of Ibiza. But it does not have the capabilities of hosting the large cruise ships with thousands of guests on board. Palma is a major city and can easily cater to the needs of multiple ships on a given day. There can be a variety of tours offered by your cruise line, either confined to the city and its immediate surroundings or extending outward to as much as a full day circumnavigation of Majorca.

If you are on a tour, you may visit only a few of the sites I note below. If you have reserved a private car and driver, you can expand your range outward and visit all of most of what I note below:

* The Cathedral of Palma - This magnificent Gothic cathedral dates to the 12th century and is a masterpiece of architectural design. It reflects the wealth and power that soon developed after the Reconquista. It is located in the heart of the city at Placa de l'Almudaina and open daily. But you should be discrete in visiting during the saying of mass.

* Bellver Castle - Located on a high hill overlooking the city, the castle offers dramatic views of Palma and much of the surrounding countryside. It was built in the 14th century for King James II of Majorca. It is of a rare design in that it is circular and has four outside battlement towers. It shape and massive size make it a major attraction, and its unusual combination of the round palace and the outside battlements make it like no other in Spain.

* Park de la Mar - Located along the waterfront just below the Cathedral and outside the old town walls, this park offers a different perspective on the city skyline as well as a green respite, especially in summer.

* Old City - Adjacent to the Cathedral is the Old City with its narrow streets, beautiful examples of Moorish and Spanish architecture and small public squares. This is one of the most beautiful of old city districts in all of Spain and should be best enjoyed on foot.

* Palau de l'Almudania - This palace adjacent to the Cathedral has been the site since Roman times for the rulers of Majorca and all of the Balearic Islands. The present buildings date to the time of the Moors, and like the Alhambra in Granada, present an excellent example of their architectural mastery.

* Basilica de Sant Francesc - This beautiful Gothic structure with its tranquil interior courtyard is a classic example of the elegant church architecture that began to be built in Palma in the 12th century. It is located in the city center at Plaza Sant Francesc 7.

* Mercat de l'Olivar - This is the main market in the city center located on Plaza del Olivar 4. It offers beautiful selections of island produce and seafood from the surrounding waters. It makes for an enjoyable stroll only if visiting a public food market is something you appreciate.

* Ferrocarril de Soller - This is a 30-kilometer or 17-mile ride on a 19th century train from the city center out into the countryside and the village of Soller. It gives you a chance to enjoy not only its antiquity, but also to glimpse the beautiful settled countryside that is so typical of Majorca.

* Playa de Palma El Arenal - This is the closest beach to the city center for those who would rather spend the day soaking up the sun and enjoying the water. There are many pubs and cafes lining this urban beach, so it is easy to enjoy the day, but of course you miss the sights.

* Serra de Tramuntana - These beautiful mountains composed primarily of limestone stretch northwest across the island. Unless a drive into these beautiful mountains is offered as a tour or you have a private car, it would be impossible to visit the mountains on your own without a rather competent taxi driver who knows the area. And it is worth seeing only if the rural landscape is of interest to you.

This listing of sights is more than sufficient for a full day on shore in Palma. For those of you who are not eager to do a lot of walking, I suggest the Old City and Cathedral areas followed by a leisurely lunch and a bit of window-shopping.

DINING OUT: Since this is only a day stop, the meal you can avail yourself of is lunch. This immediately limits the number of good restaurant choices, especially if you are looking for traditional Spanish cuisine or fresh local seafood. Here are my prime recommendations"
* Casa Jacinto - At Cicami Tranvia 27 in Genova, this is considered to be one of the finest local restaurants for lunch. It will, however, require a taxi ride unless you have a car and driver because it is not in Palma, but rather in Genova, which is in effect a suburb. The restaurant opens at 1 PM and serves very traditional Majorcan food, which includes a great variety of seafoods and meats along with elegant desserts. You will not be disappointed.
* Ola del Mar - At Calle Vicario Joaquin Fuster 1, this is another outstanding restaurant opening at 1 PM and serving delicious traditional lunches. One of their signature dishes is paella, the traditional Spanish rice and seafood dish known throughout Latin America and the Philippines as well as in Spain.
* Restaurante Peix Vermell - At Calle Montenegro 1 Bis Bajos and open from 1 PM onward, this restaurant is another excellent example of traditional cuisine served in a warm and tasteful atmosphere. Their signature dish is salt baked fish, which is delicious despite what the name implies.
* Meson Ca'n Pedro - Located at Rector Vives 14 in Genova, a visit will require a car and driver or taxi ride. Open onward from 12:30 PM, this is a meat lover's restaurant, and of course meat is very traditional in Spanish cuisine, especially away from the coast.

SHOPPING IN PALMA: As in the rest of Spain, you will find a mix of shops and major stores in the heart of Palma, but they do not specialize in arts and local crafts. Yes there are typical souvenir stores in the city center and in the Old City, and a few handcraft items will be found. The most noted shopping street in the city center is the shady Passeig des Born, a tree lined pedestrian street featuring a wide variety of shops and cafes.

IBIZA: A handful of cruise itineraries will include the Balearic Island of Ibiza as part of a western Mediterranean tour, but more often Palma de Majorca will be the port visited for this island group.

In physical size, Ibiza is the third largest of the Balearic Island, but it is still far smaller than Majorca. But it offers the same rugged beauty and far less crowding that its larger neighbor. In a similar fashion as Mykonos in the Greek Aegean islands, Ibiza has developed a rather "hip" scene with the wealthy youth of Europe who come for the cabaret nightlife and the popularity of electronic music as one of the primary forms of entertainment. But the island also offers a lot of history seen through its architecture. Ibiza Town, which is the main port, is now considered to be a UNESCO World Heritage Site because of its overall antiquity.

Like Majorca, Ibiza has been settled for millennia, having first been settled by the Phoenicians in 654 BCE. The Greeks and Romans later knew it, but it was Carthage that came to prominence, trading for the natural dyes, fish, salt and wool.

It was during the Second Punic War between Rome and Carthage in 209 BCE, the island was attacked because it had become a supply base for the Carthaginian navy. With the defeat of Carthage, Ibiza was permitted to continue to survive within the Roman Empire, but its inhabitants maintained primarily a Carthaginian lifestyle. For this reason, many of its oldest buildings date to this period, one reason it was given World Heritage status. In 990 AD, it came under Moorish control. The Muslim grip on the Balearic Islands ended in 1235 when King James I of Aragon ejected all Muslims and firmly put the islands under Christian control. In 1715, King Philip V brought the islands under firm Spanish control, taking away their semi independence.

Today the Balearic Islands are of course Spanish, but have their own degree of provincial autonomy similar to that of the Canary Islands. They are a very popular tourist getaway, especially Majorca and Menorca, but Ibiza has its strong tourist following.

VISITING IBIZA: The best way to see the island is to take one of the ship's group tours or have the shore concierge arrange a private car and driver. Otherwise you will be confined to Ibiza Town where there is not a lot to see. The primary sights worthy of note are:
* Castle of Ibiza sitting on a high hill over the port offers superb views out over an expanse of the island. The medieval castle itself is quite fascinating.

* Dalt Vila is an old village perched on the back side of the same mountain that houses the Castle of Ibiza. It is very picturesque and offers a chance to get the feel of life on the island back in the early Spanish years.
* Santa Gertrudis is a small village in the interior of the island that offers a chance to transport through a time portal to see what life was like on the island before the development of modern tourism. It is a quiet village, but it also has a few nice shops and cafes that now cater to the increased number of visitors.
* Ibiza Town Waterfront - There is a beautiful promenade and beach in the heart of Ibiza Town that although rather tourist oriented is still quite pleasant and unhurried in contrast to Palma.

DINING OUT: There are a few very nice restaurants offering lunch in Ibiza Town. Here are my recommendations:
* El Portalon - Located on Plaza des Desemparados 1 in the center of town is known for its delicious paella, which is so traditionally Spanish.
* Bistro el Jardin - On Plaza de la Constitucion 11 in the heart of town, this is a good place for a cool drink and a sampling of tapas, which can easily fill you up at lunchtime, and which is so traditionally Spanish.

SHOPPING: Ibiza Town is relatively small, but you will find nice shops carrying the same type of merchandise as seen all along the Spanish coast. And yes there are several shops containing post cards, fridge magnets, T-shirts and the usual tourist kitsch.

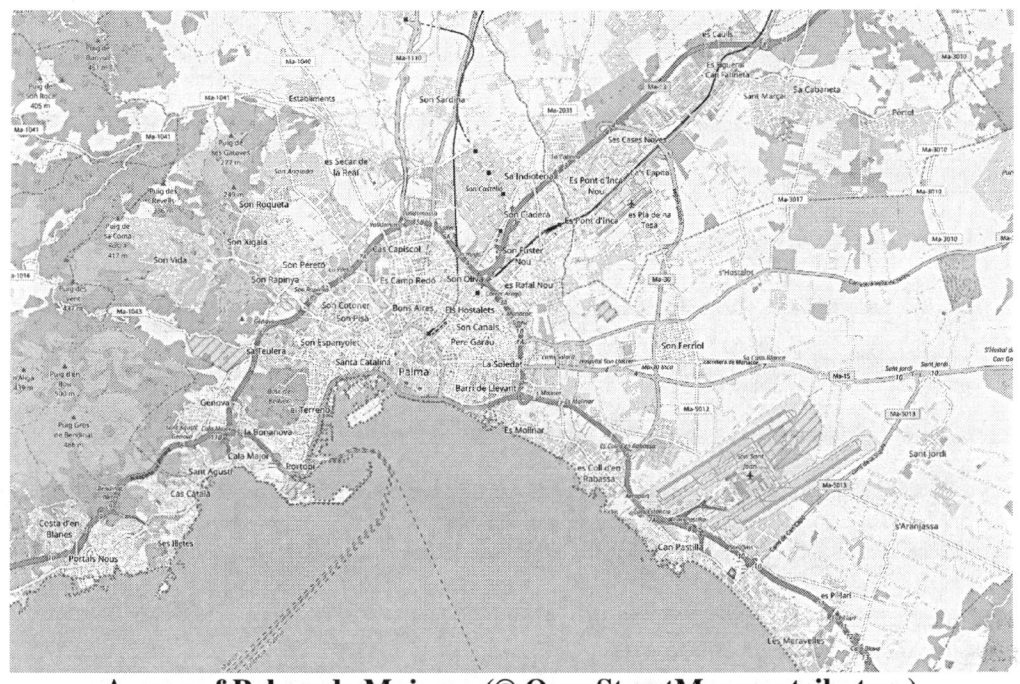

A map of Palma de Majorca (© OpenStreetMap contributors)

An aerial view of Palma (Work of Olaf Tausch, CC BY SA 3.0, Wikimedia.org)

Cathedral de Majorca in Palma (Work of Arno Ho, CC BY SA 3.0, Wikimedia.org)

The Almudaina Palace is a classic Moorish structure in Palma

Colorful old houses in the Old Town of Palma (Work of ILA boy, GNU General Public License, Wikimedia.org)

Plaça de l"Olivar in the heart of Palma (Work of Chixoy, CC BY SA 3.0, Wikimedia.org)

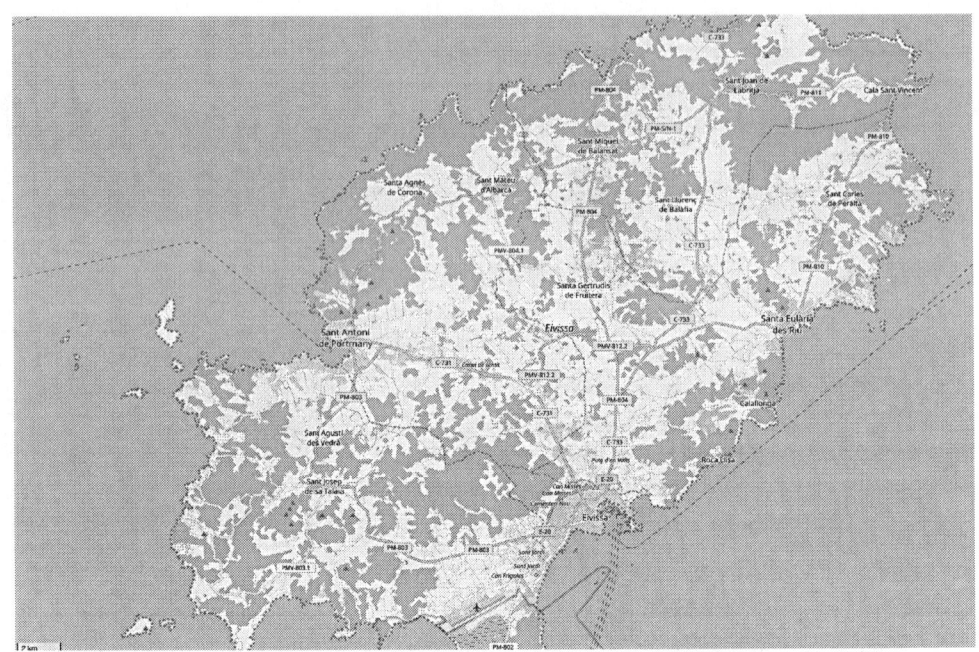

A map the small island of Ibiza (© OpenStreetMap contributors)

Overlooking the harbor in Ibiza Town (Work of XDSergio, CC BY SA 3.0, Wikimedia.org)

One of the beautiful beaches of Ibiza (Work of Kelly-ibiza, CC BY SA 3.0, Wikimedia.org)

The rugged landscape of northern Ibiza (Work of anibal amaro, CC BY SA 3.0, Wikimedia.org)

CÁDIZ: Cádiz is the major Spanish port fronting on the Atlantic Ocean. It has the distinction of being the oldest continuously inhabited city in Spain and is also one of the oldest cities along the west coast of Europe. Cadiz occupies a narrow spit of land, fronting directly on the open ocean while sheltering a large bay on its back side, which became a major port of anchorage and helped develop the city. The city is an architectural gem, its older sections being typical of the finest examples of the southern Spanish architectural flavor known as Andalusian. Old Town is generally where cruise ships dock, but unfortunately the majority of passengers choose to take a tour inland to beautiful Seville or to Jerez, therefore missing Cádiz, which is unfortunate. This is one of those ports of call where you wish the ship would overnight so you could visit both the city and still take the tour to Seville.

Most famous of all events characterizing Cádiz is the fact that on his second and fourth voyages to the New World, this is the port from which Christopher Columbus sailed. And it was to Cádiz that many exotic plants from the Americas were returned, and they have been planted in the many small parks and plazas, or at least that is what visitors are told. Although the plants may be of American origin, it is doubtful that those brought back by Columbus could still be flourishing today.

THE CITY'S HISTORY: Cádiz dates back to the ancient Phoenicians in 1100 BCE. During the First Punic War that began in 264 and ended in 241 BCE with a Carthaginian victory, they expanded their coastal hold and took control of the city so that Hannibal could use it as a major port from which to launch military incursions. By 206 BCE, Cádiz was under Roman control and its strategic importance as a port grew.

When the Visigoths overthrew Roman rule in Spain, Cádiz was totally destroyed, but the Byzantine Empire took control in 550 AD and rebuilt the city to only again loose it to the Visigoths in 572. The city fell to the Moors in 711 and their control lasted until 1262. It was under the Moors that the city was expanded as a major port. The Moorish name was Qādis from which the Spanish name Cádiz derives.

After the Spanish took control, it became a major port with the development of the colonial empire in the New World, best known historically as the port used by Christopher Columbus for two of his voyages. As a result of the founding of the major Spanish colonies, conquest of the Aztec and Inca Empires and the exploitation of the riches of the New World, Cádiz became the major port for what became known as Spain's "Treasure Fleet," a target of privateers and pirates for decades. Not only were the ships major targets for raids, but so was the city of Cádiz all through the 16th century. The most famous attack was by Sir Francis Drake of England who captured and/or destroyed a large number of Spanish galleons. It is said that Drake's attack set back Spain's plans to conquer England with its vast armada that was finally defeated by the British in 1588.

Because Cádiz was the major port for Andalusia, the richest part of Spain, it became victim of further English attacks, one in 1596 when the city was heavily looted, and again in 1625. But at least that attack was essentially thwarted. Later the city was blockaded from 1655 to 1657 by the British, and in 1702, the British were beaten back in a very bloody event known as the Battle of Cádiz.

The rival port of Seville, which is inland along the Guadalquivir River was finally put out of action by the clogging of the river by massive silt deposits. This now left Cádiz as the major port for all trade with the Latin American colonies. This gave a tremendous boost to the city's economy and actually is spoken of as the "golden age" of wealth and development for Cádiz.

Once again the British blockaded Cádiz during the Napoleonic Wars. During the Peninsular War against Napoleonic forces, Cádiz was able to hold off the French forces because of its somewhat isolated geographic position. It became the capital of Spain in exile, home to the parliament as well as the military. And at the end of the war in 1812, it was here that the new Spanish Constitution was announced.

When the new constitution was renounced by Ferdinand VII, the revolutionaries of Cádiz managed to hold the king prisoner in 1823, but with French military help they were forced to relinquish their control and free the monarch. Later in 1868, the revolutionary forces of Cádiz managed to force the abdication of Queen Isabella II, but the monarchy was returned to more limited power in 1870. Thus the city of Cádiz has played a very active role in the royal history of Spain.

SIGHTSEEING: Cádiz is a city worthy of your attention. If you choose to visit Seville, you will of course be exploring one of the great and magnificent cities of Spain, as will be noted in the next section. But if you stay in Cádiz, you will be equally rewarded, as this small city is so full of history and offers so much architectural flavor. Old Town Cádiz where most cruise ships dock is relatively small, as the peninsula is narrow and elongated. All the major sights you will want to see are within a radius of less than two kilometers or one mile from the cruise port. Only the new, modern part of the city is a bit too far for most people to visit on foot. But of course most cruise lines will offer tours of Cádiz, both the older and new parts of the city.

Here are my recommendations as to what should not be missed when exploring the city of Cádiz:
* Cathedral of Cadiz - Given the wealth of this once great port, the Cathedral of Cádiz expresses the splendor of a house of worship that was patronized by a rich merchant, military and noble class. It is in the heart of Barrio del Populo, the old heart of the city and fronts on a beautiful plaza.
* Barrio del Populo - This is the maze of narrow streets making up the heart of the old part of Cádiz. It is an area in which you can walk for hours to just savor the beautiful architecture. Many of the great homes of wealthy shippers also had tall towers from which they could survey the harbor, and also seek protection during attack. Several are open to groups on walking tours.
* Museum of Cádiz - Located at the far end of the peninsula in the older city at Plaza de Mina and open from 9 AM to 8 PM, this museum presents excellent artifacts and descriptions of the long history of this famous city. I recommend it for anyone with a keen historic interest.
* Plaza de las Flores - This plaza in the older part of the city is home to numerous flower shops, cafes and is dominated over by a large statue of Columbus. It is one of the main plazas in the heart of Cádiz.
* San Juan de Dios Square - This is the most major square in the older part of Cádiz and the only way to describe it is to say it is stunning. This is Spanish architecture at its finest.
* Plaza Libertad and the Mercado Central - Located on this major plaza is the city's expansive public food market. It is a good lesson in Spanish cuisine as well as being highly colorful and worthy of a visit.
* Parc Genoves - At the far end of the peninsula and facing the open Atlantic along Avenida Doctor Gomez Ulla is a beautiful park that is said to feature many plants brought back from the Americas. After walking to the end of the peninsula, this is also a great place for a respite amid its lush greenery.
* Paseo Canalejas - The outer walk along oceanfront you have a great view of the city skyline and the crashing surf on the Atlantic side of the peninsula. This is a popular place for locals to stroll.
* Castillo de Santa Catalina - This is one of the forts facing the Atlantic whose guns helped try to keep the city safe, but was not always successful.
* Castillo de San Sebastián - This is the larger of the two major fortresses that helped keep the city as safe as possible. The fortress is on a small island connected to the mainland by a causeway and it offers great views of the city of Cádiz.

DINING OUT: The sights noted above are sufficient to keep you busy for most of the day, but of course you must take time to enjoy a tantalizing lunch in one of the beautiful restaurants of Cádiz. My choices for lunch are:

* El Garbanzo Negro - Located on Calle Sacramento 18, and open from Noon to 5 Pm for lunch, this is a traditional Spanish restaurant with excellent food served in a sedate and quiet atmosphere. Their food combines tastes from Spain with those from across the water in Morocco.

* La Candela - Located at Calle Feduchy 3 in the older city and open from 1:30 to 4 PM, again offering excellent food and quiet atmosphere. They serve quite an array of meats and seafood and also vegetarian dishes.

* Restaurante Cafe Royalty - Located in a restored classic building at Plaza de la Candalaria and open from 9 AM to Midnight, serving very traditional Spanish cuisine expertly prepared.

SHOPPING: There is no central downtown in the older parts of the city, but there are shops selling all variety of merchandise around every plaza and on all the major streets of the city. Again the merchandise is what you will see all across Spain, but Cádiz does offer some shops that specialize in typical Andalusian handcrafts such as pottery, glass, leather and embroidery.

SEVILLE:
Seville, better known in English as Seville is another one of those cities in Andalusia that has a "magical" quality about it similar to that described for Granada. Seville is located inland from the coast along the banks of the Guadalquivir River that was once navigable in the days of the sailing vessels. Thus its early history is tied to the sea, as the city was an important port. Today the city of Cádiz serves as its primary port when in the past they were essentially rivals for overseas trade.

Today Seville is a major city with a population of just over 1,500,000 in its metropolitan area, yet it has maintained a large inner city core that is historically charming and enticing to visitors because of its exquisite Moorish and Spanish architecture. Four square kilometers of the inner city comprises a very important historic zone that is today a UNESCO World Heritage Site. In ranking with other Spanish cities population wise, Seville is the fourth largest city in the country.

The climate of the lands surrounding Seville is typically Mediterranean with the usual pattern of mild, wet winters and hot and dry summers. Many sources show the city to have the highest average summer temperatures of any city in Europe, averaging well above 30 degrees Celsius or 88 degrees Fahrenheit. The land around Seville is very productive, known for its sour oranges, grapes, other fruits and a wide array of vegetables. Seville oranges are the primary ingredient in orange marmalade, a very popular breakfast condiment in much of Europe, especially in the United Kingdom and Ireland.

To appreciate the architectural significance of Seville and to understand why it is such a magnet for cruise tourists when they land in Cádiz, it is necessary to have a brief review of this city's history.

A SHORT HISTORY: Seville is a very old city, dating back over 2,200 years ago. Phoenician traders are credited with the original founding of the city. However, there is a strong mythological story that claims Hercules is responsible for its creation.

During the Roman occupancy of southern Spain, Seville was an important trade center, as evidenced by many surviving remains, including part of an aqueduct, parts of the ancient city wall and several buildings. Following the fall of Rome, the Vandals and Visigoths occupied the city prior to the major invasion of the Moors.

The Moors conquered most of southern Spain by 712 AD, and Seville became capital for three of the most powerful Islamic dynasties, each ruling in succession. The Moors left a deep footprint with regard to architecture. Much of what has come to be recognized as southern Spanish architecture - houses built around a courtyard with its splashing fountain and plantings of greenery is actually of Moorish origin, but it came to be the favored style by the Spanish after the Reconquista, but less so in the interior than in Andalusia.

In 1278, Christian forces created a condition where surrender was necessary after the main bridge connecting the city with its vital hinterland was incapacitated. Had it not surrendered it would have starved. Once conquered, Seville became a major center for religious activities and government. Although the Spanish quickly showed a taste for the Moorish style, the great Seville Cathedral was built in the magnificence of the Gothic motif. But many of the Moorish palaces became home to Spanish nobility with few changes to the style of the buildings.

At the time of the Reconquista, Seville had a large Jewish population in addition to its Muslim majority. The Spanish forced the majority of Muslims to flee, but Jews were initially tolerated. But 1391 marked the start of a series of persecutions aimed at the Jewish community. In 1478, the Inquisition came to Seville, and Jews were among its major targets. By 1492, Jews either had to convert to Catholicism or flee the country. Many did convert, but the majority fled to the Middle East where they became recognized as the Sephardic Jews, still found in many countries of the region today.

As the American colonies of Spain quickly grew during the early and mid 1500's, Seville held the Royal monopoly on trade, and as a result the city grew in wealth and power. It was when Cádiz also received a Royal charter and the Guadalquivir River began to silt up that so-called "golden age" of wealth and power came crashing down on the city.

The city recovered some of its economic prowess in the 18th century when the king actually encouraged manufacturing activities. The city also became an important center of education and the arts. This trend continued into the 19th and 20th centuries along with improvements to and modernization of its infrastructure of roads, railways, bridges and public spaces. In 1929, Seville was the host city for the Ibero-American Exposition, which brought a resurgence of the Moorish and Spanish architectural style, especially in the building of the Plaza de España, which is one of the city's major gems today.

Today tourism plays a major role along with manufacturing, banking and education. The city has maintained its magnificent inner core that is celebrated as an architectural gem. At the same time, it has modern expressways and also high-speed rail service to Madrid.

SIGHTSEEING: Although I will note the major sights, if you are on a group tour, you may or may not see all or most of what I recommend. However, if you have a private car and driver, then at least my list can help you plan. But always rely as well upon the knowledge of your driver/guide.

Here are my recommendations of the top sights to see in Seville:
* Catedral de Sevilla - Located in the heart of the older part of the city, this is one of the most spectacular and magnificent cathedrals in all of Europe. It was built in the 15th century, part of it having preexisted under Moorish rule, and later incorporated into the overall Gothic design. Its tower known as La Giralda was originally a minaret, and it offers the most spectacular views of the city. It also houses an interior garden of very old orange trees.
* Centro Historico is one of the oldest sections of the city and it houses many fine churches, palaces and also a plethora of narrow streets and small houses and shops. It is a very captivating part of the old city.
* Plaza de Triunfo is the main plaza outside of the Cathedral and it affords fantastic views of the main house of worship that is the centerpiece of the old city. And it is also a great place for people watching.
* Real Alcazar located in the city center is the old Moorish and later Spanish royal residence with a mixture of Moorish and Spanish architectural flavors. And its large garden it absolutely stunning and a must see sight. The palace is open from 9:30 AM to 7 PM.

* Plaza de España and Parque de Maria Luisa are two adjacent sites that date back to 1929 and the Ibero Americana Exhibition. Plaza de España is a magnificent semi circular building with fanciful archways that combine Gothic and Moorish style. A boat ride on the small lake gives you a chance to savor the architecture without so many people in your field of view. Remember that this is a contemporary construct meant to look like a piece of antiquity.
* Museo del Baile Flamenco - Located on Avenida Manuel Rojas Marcos 3, this is an excellent place to learn about the Andalusian dance form known as flamenco that is so popular throughout Spain. It is open from 9:30 AM to 7 PM and often has demonstration performances.
* Casa de Pilatos - At Plaza Pilatos 1 in the city center, this is a noble palace that was built starting in 1492. The architecture and decor mix Roman, Moorish and Spanish elements. The palace is also part museum and well worth a visit.
* Basilica de la Macarena at Calle de Becquer 1 is a fine example of the many large cathedrals honoring various saints and Madonnas. This basilica is home to the statue of the Virgin of Hope and figures prominently in a major procession during Holy Week leading to Easter.

I will not make note of places to dine because Seville is not a port of call. If you visit, it will be either on a group tour or with a private car and driver. On group tours lunch is included and you have no choice as to restaurant or menu selection. If you visit on your own with a car and driver, it is best to rely upon his/her knowledge of the city for recommendations. And you will also not have any specific time for real shopping since there are so many sights to behold in your short time in Seville.

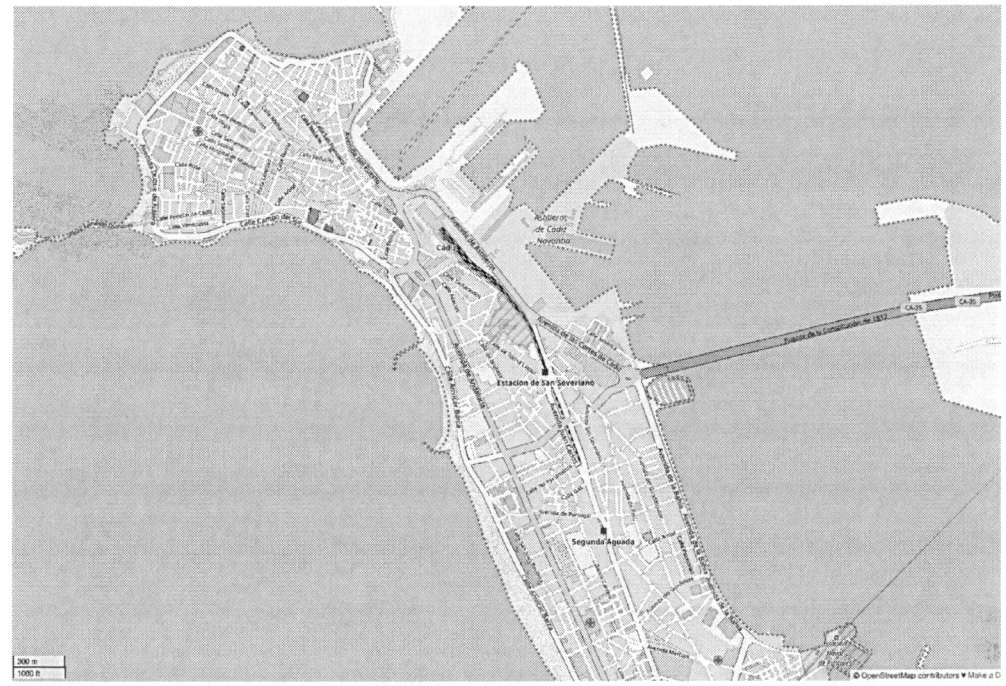

A map of the city of Cádiz (© OpenStreetMap contributors)

A view over the center of Cádiz (Work of Panarria, CC BY SA 3.0, Wikimedia.org)

The great Cathedral of Cádiz

Plaza San Juan de Dios in the heart of Cádiz

One of the major shopping streets near the Cathedral

Old Narrow streets off of Avenida Ramon de Carranza

In the vicinity of the Mercado Central

Inside the Mercado Central

Along Campo del Sur facing the open Atlantic Ocean

The Independence Monument of Cádiz

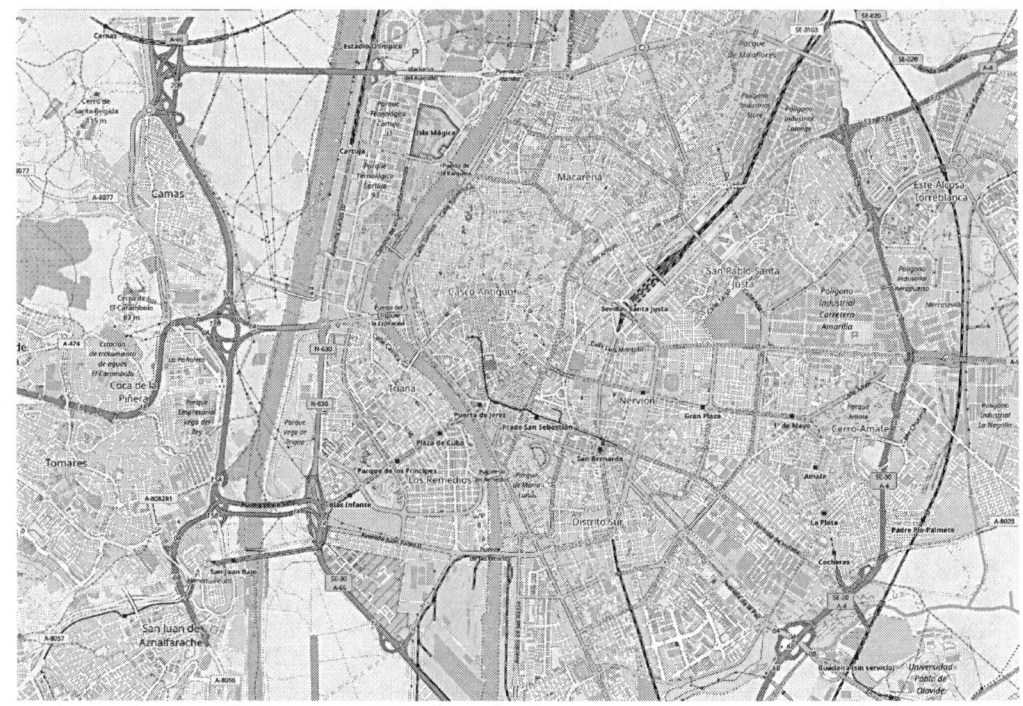

A map of the city of Seville (© OpenStreetMap contributors)

Flying over Seville (Work of El-Mejor, CC BY SA 3.0, Wikimedia.org)

The skyline of Seville from the Cathedral (Work of José Luiz Bernardes Ribeiro, CC BY SA 3.0, Wikimedia.org)

Looking down on the grand cathedral (Work of Michal Osmenda, CC BY SA 2.0, Wikimedia.org)

The Cathedral of Seville close up (Work of Ingo Mehling, CC BY SA 4.0, Wikimedia.org)

The gardens of the Alcazar (Work of José Luis Filpo Cabaña, CC BY SA 3.0, Wikimedia.org)

Inside the Palace of the Dueñas (Work of Benjamin Nuñez Gonzáles, CC BY SA 4.0, Wikimedia.org)

Plaza de España in València

FINAL WRAP UP

Now we come to the end of this cruise guide to the western Mediterranean. As you can see by this point, there is a lot to absorb when it comes to the different ports of call that can go into an itinerary for the western part of the Mediterranean Sea, often including a few stops on the Atlantic margins of Spain, Portugal and on occasion Morocco.

There is a lot of rich historical detail to absorb, and there is a lot of beautiful countryside combining both the natural and human elements. The Mediterranean Sea captivates millions every year. Of course it is so large and expansive that one single cruise could never begin to do it justice. Even if you had the time and the money to do a 30-day cruise from one end to the other, you would develop so much sensory overload that it would be hard to remember all you have seen. On my first visit to the Mediterranean I cruised all the way from Athens to Lisbon, which took over 18 days with all of the stops. And it was too much even for a professional geographer, as each country is different and after a week, the flavors become jumbled together. The best way to see the Mediterranean Sea is to take multiple cruises, doing only one section at a time, and never spending more than 10 days or two weeks, but still only in one major sector.

There will be two more editions to compliment this first book. There will be a book on the central Mediterranean, which will encompass Italy, the islands of Corsica (French) and Sardinia (Italian), Malta and Tunisia. And there will be a third volume that will include ports of call in Croatia, Montenegro, Greece, Turkey, Cyprus, Israel and Egypt. Syria and Lebanon are not going to be included because of the raging conflict that has made both countries far too dangerous to visit. No cruise line at present includes any ports in either country.

I trust this book will be helpful in planning your western Mediterranean cruise.

ABOUT THE AUTHOR

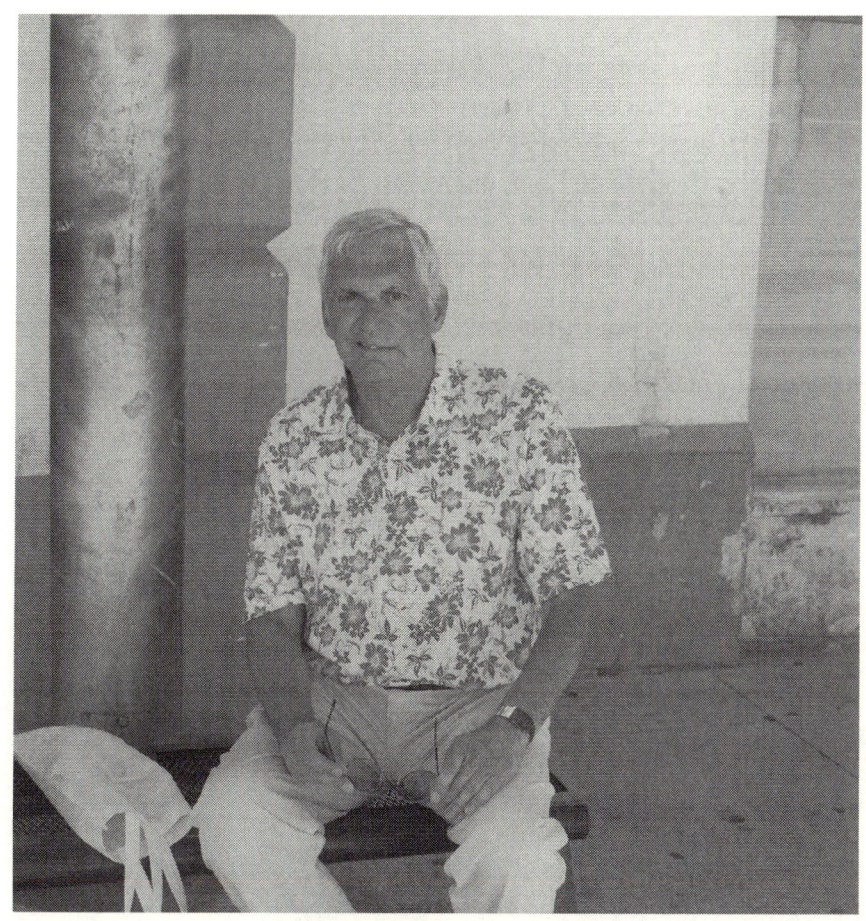

Dr. Lew Deitch

I am a Canadian-American dual citizen who is a semi-retired professor of geography with over 46 years of teaching experience. During my distinguished career, I directed the Honors Program at Northern Arizona University and developed many programs relating to the study of contemporary world affairs. I am an honors graduate of The University of California, Los Angeles, earned my Master of Arts at The University of Arizona and completed my doctorate in geography at The University of New England in Australia. I am a globetrotter, having visited 96 countries on all continents except Antarctica. My primary focus is upon human landscapes, especially such topics as local architecture, foods, clothing and folk music. I am also a student of world politics and conflict.

I enjoy being in front of an audience, and have spoken to thousands of people at civic and professional organizations. I have been lecturing on board ships for a major five star cruise line since 2008. I love to introduce people to exciting new places both by means of presenting vividly illustrated talks and through serving as a tour consultant for ports of call. I am also an avid writer, and for years I have written my own text books used in my university classes. Now I have turned my attention to writing travel companions, books that will introduce you to the country you are visiting, but not serving as a touring book like the major guides you find in all of the bookstores.

I also love languages, and my skills include a conversational knowledge of German, Russian and Spanish.

Arizona has been his permanent home since 1974. One exciting aspect of my life was the ten-year period, during which I volunteered my time as an Arizona Highway Patrol reserve trooper, working out on the streets and highways and also developing new safety and enforcement programs for use statewide. I presently live just outside of Phoenix in the beautiful resort city of Scottsdale and still offer a few courses for the local community colleges when I am at home.

I would like to extend an invitation for you to join me on one of the Silversea cruise segments when I am on board presenting my destination talks. You would find it to be a wonderful experience, especially after having read my book on this area, or on the others I have written about.

FOR MORE INFORMATION REGARDING TRAVELING ON BOARD WHEN I AM THE SPEAKER, CONTACT, WESTSIDE INTERNATIONAL TRAVEL, THE TRAVEL AGENCY I USE FOR ALL MY TRAVELS AT:

www.westsideintltravel.com

TO CONTACT ME, PLEASE CHECK OUT MY WEB PAGE FOR MORE INFORMATION AT:

http://www.doctorlew.com

Made in the USA
San Bernardino, CA
05 January 2019